- *Under what circumsta* ——— *Party in 1921?*

- *What is the origin of the swastika?*

- *How did Hitler come to write the chaotic tract* Mein Kampf?

- *What was Hitler's true relationship with Eva Braun? With his parents? His siblings?*

- *What were the foundations of his anti-Semitic obsessions?*

- *What was contained in Hitler's will?*

The rumors. The facts. The myths. The truth.

"FASCINATING READING."
—*Booklist*

A Concise Biography of Adolf Hitler

THOMAS FUCHS

Previously published as The Hitler Fact Book

BERKLEY BOOKS, NEW YORK

A CONCISE BIOGRAPHY OF ADOLF HITLER

A Berkley Book / published by arrangement with
the author

PRINTING HISTORY
Fountain Books trade paperback edition published in 1990
as *The Hitler Fact Book*
Berkley edition / February 2000

The Penguin Putnam Inc. World Wide Web site address is
http://www.penguinputnam.com

ISBN: 0-425-17340-2

BERKLEY®
Berkley Books are published by The Berkley Publishing Group,
a division of Penguin Putnam Inc.,
375 Hudson Street, New York, New York 10014.
BERKLEY and the ''B'' design
are trademarks belonging to Penguin Putnam Inc.

PRINTED IN THE UNITED STATES OF AMERICA

Contents

PREFACE

How to Use This Book, and Why

Was Hitler really a vegetarian? Is it true he helped design the Volkswagen? Was he homosexual? Did he consult with astrologers before making decisions?

For the foreseeable future, for better or worse, stories will be told about Hitler, assertions made. He and his hideous career are regularly invoked on subjects ranging from health food to mass murder. A book like this one may therefore serve as a useful reference, providing quick access to reliable information.

But the book has a larger purpose—to make Hitler real. To some degree he has already become a legendary creature, rather like Dracula or Frankenstein's Monster, the stuff of horror movies and comedies. Although we might prefer a Hitler cast out from the human race, it would be foolishness of the most dangerous kind to remove him from the flow of history and ignore the potential for evil that exists in all populations and institutions.

Popular interest in Hitler never flags, and since this book first appeared in 1990, the stream of books and articles about him and Nazi Germany has only grown. There have been no great discoveries, no new facts that might alter the story but particular authors continue to bring their particular sensibilities to bear on different aspects of Hitler's life.

In 1997, the distinguished historian John Lukacs published *The Hitler of History*, a book which, in large part, is actually about books on Hitler. Lukacs demonstrates that there can be no single, objective account of the man and the monstrous history he made. The subject is too complex and all who write about Hitler either begin with or develop a point of view, which shapes their account; for example, was Hitler a natural consequence of the German history preceding him or an aberration?

Some of Hitler's biographers have argued that Hitler was little more than a power-hungry opportunist; others, that he was driven by psychosexual obsessions; still others, that he was a man of ideas genuinely bent on transforming Europe and the world. Lukacs himself has an argument to make. Although Hitler is often portrayed as a reactionary determined to return the world to some vaguely defined pre-modern condition, Lukacs believes he was actually a revolutionary, inspired and abetted by social, political and intellectual changes unleashed in the modern world. Perhaps most importantly, Lukacs refutes those historians who, in their portrayal of Hitler and his historical context, have sought to exonerate him or minimize his personal responsibility. The fact that circumstances favored his rise does not absolve Hitler of his enormous guilt.

In 1998, the essayist and novelist Ron Rosenbaum published *Explaining Hitler*, an account of his own attempt to understand Hitler's character—how it formed; indeed, what was its real nature? For example, did Hitler kill only because he believed murder was necessary to accomplish his ends, or did he revel in it, finding exultation in destruction and death?

The dust jacket of Rosenbaum's book features Hitler's baby picture, an image that signifies the mystery that so intrigues Rosenbaum. How could someone born of flesh and blood do what Hitler did? After reading numerous books, Rosenbaum visited with scholars who have spent their lives studying and writing about Hitler. The result is a series of fascinating interviews. Inevitably the question of evil arises: Does evil exist apart from evil acts? Is it only an adjective or does it name something—perhaps an inchoate, incomplete form of human nature?

A Concise Biography of Adolf Hitler does not venture into speculation or abstraction. I believe it continues to be of value because it serves a simpler function, providing concrete details and anecdotes in an easily accessible format. Readers can peruse it straight through or, guided by the contents and index, go directly to areas and items of immediate interest. No matter what the approach, the reader will soon confront the malevolent storm of Hitler's soul—his hatred of Jews, his warmongering, the unremitting drive to dominate the world and everyone in it.

A reader who finds a particular item literally incredible or wishes to pursue it more thoroughly can check the notes and sources section beginning on page 197. This is keyed to the bibliography, which follows it.

Because the book is organized by subject areas rather than dates, readers interested in the sequence of events might wish to refer to the chronology, which starts on page 245.

There is no surer way to pull the cloak of mystery from a man than to provide a physical description of him, in this case beginning with that feature which is so emblematic of him—his mustache.

ONE

Hitler's Mustache

. . . the ridiculous little smudge which made him look as if he had not cleaned his nose.

—E. HANFSTAENGL

Hitler's mustache was a traditional type, but even among his supporters it was thought to look absurd and ugly on him. In 1923, Ernst Hanfstaengl, a close associate, suggested he let it grow out to the ends of his lips. Trying to be tactful, he told Hitler—leader of a Nazi Party that was still obscure and weak—that the short brush style was unfashionable.

Hitler's response was characteristic. "If it is not the fashion now, it will be later," he said, "because I wear it."

Anecdotes like this may help make Hitler accessible—if not fully understandable—and this is necessary because the very enormity of his crimes leads to his often being represented as either sub-human or as a supernatural figure, a demon. Both misconceptions are dangerous. They make him unreal, with the possible consequence of our forgetting that what he did can be done again.

1

It is for the sake of seeing Hitler just as he was that
this collection of anecdotes and facts has been assembled.

The source material is abundant, enormous. Probably
no one in history has been more closely observed and
reported on. There is even an account of how he cultivated the famous forelock which, like his mustache, was
an essential identifying element of his appearance. After
the war, one of his secretaries described the procedure
to an Allied interrogator:

> He would bend over forward and comb his hair
> down before his eyes just like a woman does, then
> he would make the part and just loosely comb
> back the left portion so that with a jerk of the head
> the left forward lock would drop over his fore-
> head—and this happened all the time during his
> speech making.

Hitler's hair was dark brown, almost black. His collar
and shoulders were often flecked with dandruff.

The Hypnotic Stare

Hitler's eyes were blue, or blue-gray. An officer who
worked at Headquarters during the war made the remarkable observation that Hitler sometimes crossed
them, "in jest."

By the time Hitler was in his late forties, he had become farsighted. Reports sent to him had to be typed
out on a "Fuehrer typewriter," the letters of which were
about twice normal size, (almost half an inch high).

He regularly used eyeglasses and although he was photographed wearing them, publication of these photographs was forbidden. Some have survived, however, including one with an X through it, made on the proof sheet by Hitler himself.

Hitler's eyes are important historically because of the mystical qualities sometimes attributed to them; followers frequently describe them as blazing, hypnotic, dominating. In objective fact, they were physically prominent—large and slightly bulging—and Hitler made a point of using them for dramatic effect.

It was his practice, when meeting someone for the first time, to stare with what he imagined to be a penetrating gaze. Not surprisingly, this made a profound impression on many visitors, especially those who had come to the interview wanting this to be their unforgettable meeting with the self-described "greatest German of all time."

Others found the famous stare "opaque, dull."

Hitler's Head

Hitler's head was not remarkable, although he thought it was. In February 1937 he summoned a distinguished surgeon, Professor Ferdinand Sauerbruck, and a team of phrenologists to take measurements of his skull. These experts concluded that the various dimensions of Hitler's head (*e.g.* the distance from chin to forehead, from eye socket to eye socket, and so on) were: "Just like Napoleon's" and "Nothing like it since Frederick the Great!"

Hitler was delighted and had their findings written up

in a 130 page manuscript which was carefully stored in his private library.

Phrenology—the attempt to correlate skull measurements with intelligence and character—fitted in well with Nazi ideas about racial superiority, but of course this "science" is no science at all. The conclusions of any particular investigation seemed to depend almost entirely on the investigator's preconceived ideas. In 1924, when Hitler was on trial for his failed early attempt to seize the government, the prosecution produced Max von Gruber, Professor of something called "racial hygiene," who testified that Hitler's features demonstrated, "bad race, mongrel. Low receding forehead, ugly nose, broad cheekbones, small eyes, dark hair . . ."

Height and Weight

For some reason, a common myth circulates to the effect that Hitler was abnormally short. In fact, he was just under five feet, ten inches.

He weighed about 155 pounds, but this is necessarily only an estimate. Hitler could not be weighed as an ordinary patient would because his personal peculiarities included a refusal to undress for medical examinations. According to one of his doctors, "Hitler had an extreme disinclination to let people see his body. Even I never saw him completely unclothed, let alone checked him over in that state."

A wartime Allied song began, "Hitler, he only has one ball . . ." Since then, perhaps hundreds of pages have been written in serious debate as to whether or not there was anything unusual about Hitler's genitals, often focusing on the possibility that he may indeed have had only one testicle. The debate has not been conclusive.

General Constitution

Although inclined to hypochondria, Hitler in middle age was a vigorous man with ruddy cheeks and excellent endurance.

There was an ominous significance to his good health, particularly because it was linked to his fear of physical decline. Despite repeated public assurances that he desired peace, he said something else to his Generals on April 20, 1939, the day he turned fifty. He told them he wanted to fight a war soon, while he was still strong. As the years passed, he explained, he would lose the stamina war required.

Less than five months later, on September 1, he invaded Poland and began World War II. (Franklin Roosevelt was fifty-seven; Winston Churchill, sixty-five.)

TWO

Hitler's Dog

I love animals, and especially dogs.

—HITLER

The man who murdered millions sometimes seemed capable of normal affection, but in everything he did, Hitler ultimately revealed an utter indifference to any life but his own. The sad story of his dog Blondi illustrates the point.

Hitler was fond of dogs and was rarely without one. In 1941, Martin Bormann, a top aide, sought to ingratiate himself by giving his Fuehrer a magnificent German shepherd bitch named Blondi.

The gift was a great success. Hitler enthusiastically began teaching Blondi tricks. Soon she could fetch, jump through hoops, clear a six-foot fence, even climb a stepladder and beg. On special occasions, Hitler would have her "sing" for guests.

Hitler became devoted to Blondi. Delighted when he thought she was pregnant, he was deeply disappointed when he realized she was merely overweight.

Blondi always slept in Hitler's bedroom, in her special

wooden box. An Army sergeant named Tornow was detailed to attend to her full-time.

Whenever Hitler traveled, Blondi went with him, to
his mountain villa, to the government Chancellery in
Berlin, to his various military headquarters. And when
the tide of war finally turned against the Nazis, Blondi—
in a twist possible only in the kind of state Hitler had
created—began to assume enormous importance.

With the German front in Russia in danger of complete collapse, Hitler's Generals wanted desperately to
withdraw and consolidate their forces, but Hitler would
have none of this. He was rigid in his strategy—no re-
treat, ever. The Generals were frantic, and then they realized Blondi offered an opportunity.

During even the most pressing military crises, Hitler
took breaks between conferences, to walk Blondi and
put her through her tricks. The Generals, who often went
along, discovered that when Blondi performed well, Hitler mellowed, and in these brief periods of good humor
would sometimes take their advice. Of course, if Blondi
didn't do well, Hitler remained intractable. One of the
officers later recalled, "I sometimes had the impression
that the outcome of the Russian campaign depended
more upon Blondi than the German general staff."

Despite Blondi (or perhaps she really wasn't very capable), the German armies were steadily torn to pieces.
In time, as the Russians closed in on Berlin, Hitler
moved into his bomb-proof bunker beneath the Chancellery garden, from which he continued to issue orders
and battle plans, concocting elaborate but completely

groundless schemes for turning the cataclysmic defeat into victory.

Blondi, meanwhile, had managed to give birth to five pups, specially accommodated in a kennel built for them in the bunker. Of the litter, Hitler was particularly taken by one he dubbed Wolf, a favorite nickname. No one but Hitler was allowed to touch Wolf. He would stroke the pup with great tenderness, murmuring its name over and over.

Finally, even Hitler had to admit the war was lost. There was only one defeat left, and this he was determined to avoid. He had a morbid fear of being captured alive by the Russians, imagining among other things that they might put him on exhibit in a cage in Moscow. His recourse was suicide.

He intended to use cyanide, supplied in small glass ampules by the S.S. But then the unthinkable happened. The S.S. was headed by Heinrich Himmler ("the faithful Heinrich," Hitler called him), and Hitler learned that Himmler, operating out of reach in the north, was trying to open independent peace negotiations with the Allies. That made him a traitor.

Hitler quickly came to the conclusion that the cyanide supplied by Himmler's S.S. might not be cyanide at all. Perhaps it was only a knockout drug. Perhaps Himmler was planning to deliver him unconscious but alive to the Russians, for cash or favor. The cyanide had to be tested.

Hitler chose Blondi for the test.

Sergeant Tornow, Blondi's keeper, and a doctor named Haase took the dog into the bathroom. There, Tornow held her jaws open while Haase used a pair of pliers to push the ampule to the back of her mouth. Then he squeezed, breaking the capsule and releasing the cyanide.

After it was over, the ever suspicious Hitler came into the bathroom to make sure Blondi was dead. He said nothing and his face displayed no emotion. Then he returned to his study, to continue planning his suicide.

Soon after, for some reason which is not recorded, Sergeant Tornow shot the pups.

THREE

Mein Kampf, Hitler's Book

Hitler's first battle was with the German language, and this fight, at least, he has not won.

—DOROTHY THOMPSON, 1939

To learn about a man's mind, it is usually instructive to study what he has written—but Hitler wrote a book so long and incoherent few people have been able to read it. Nevertheless, it made him a millionaire.

The book is *Mein Kampf*, and much of it was written in jail.

In 1924, Hitler was serving a sentence in Landsberg Fortress for his attempt to overthrow the government in the so-called Beer Hall Putsch. This violent, blatantly illegal episode had resulted in the deaths of sixteen Nazis and three policemen, but key members of the government secretly sympathized with Hitler's aims and he was treated well at Landsberg. Many jail personnel regularly greeted him with "Heil Hitler!"; admirers sent so many gifts his suite of rooms began to look like a cross between a delicatessen and a flower shop.

Hitler was not alone in his confinement. Other top Nazis rounded up after the failed overthrow were also given rooms there. Although imprisoned, life was not unpleasant except for one problem—Hitler's endless harangues. Hour after hour, he talked on and on about his ideas, his plans, his destiny, himself. Then one of the prisoners had an ingenious idea. He urged Hitler not to waste these precious words. Instead of merely speaking them, why not save them for posterity by writing them down? Why not write a book?

Hitler promptly borrowed a Remington typewriter from the prison warden and set to work, dictating to his chauffeur, Emil Maurice, who typed. (Maurice was soon replaced by Rudolf Hess.) Hitler later said he was spurred on by the heavy clacking of the Remington's keys. And by the music. A gramophone played intoxicating, heroic Wagner records over and over as Hitler paced and ranted.

By the time of his early release "for good behavior" at the end of 1924, the book was well under way. Although it was eventually published as *Mein Kampf* (which means "My Struggle"), this was not Hitler's original title. Until he was dissuaded by his publisher, he had planned to call his book: *Four and a Half Years of Struggle Against Lies, Stupidity and Cowardice*.

Mein Kampf is a vicious book—chaotic and vile, like the mind of its author. In it, Hitler expounds the idea that the German people are a superior race who ought to rule the world; he calls for a war to defeat France and her allies and for German colonization of much of Russia.

Jews are depicted as engaged in a systematic attempt to corrupt and wreck all that is civilized and decent. Among Jewish tactics, we are told, is the raping of

German women in order to poison good German blood.

Hitler got much of his anti-Semitic ideas—including the grotesque sexuality—from tracts he had read in his youth. Similarly, the section of *Mein Kampf* devoted to the uses of propaganda was largely lifted from other sources (see chapter 17, "Hitler's Bookshelf").

The autobiography in *Mein Kampf* is largely untrue.

Hitler's book was not a big seller at first but after he became Chancellor in 1933 it became required reading—or at least a required ornament—in almost every German home and office, as well as a *de rigueur* graduation present. Ultimately, a law was passed requiring every municipality in the land to buy and give a copy to each new married couple.

Hitler received an author's royalty, and *Mein Kampf* soon made him a multimillionaire. The process was hastened somewhat when he ordered the publisher (a Nazi firm) to raise his royalty from the customary ten percent of the cover price to fifteen.

Although tens of millions of copies of *Mein Kampf* were sold, its style was so convoluted and repetitious even dedicated Nazis couldn't get through it. One of them, Otto Strasser, picked out a few short passages and quoted them in a speech he gave at a Party rally in 1927. The Fuehrer's words were applauded vigorously. Later, at a dinner *not* attended by Hitler, some of Strasser's colleagues asked if he had actually read *Mein Kampf*. When he admitted he had not, everyone else at the table confessed the same shortcoming. More diners were expected, so those already present made a secret agreement. As each new diner arrived—and all were veteran, top-ranking Nazis—he would be asked if he had read

the great work. The first who claimed he had managed
the task would be stuck with the dinner check for all.
One of the men on whom this trap was sprung was Hermann Goering, the fat future Air Force chief and second
in command to Hitler. He responded to the question by
laughing out loud. Even Joseph Goebbels, future head
of Propaganda for the Third Reich, admitted (with some
show of guilt) that he had been unable to get through
Hitler's book. At the evening's end, reports Strasser,
each diner had to pay his own check. None of them had
actually read *Mein Kampf*.

Of course, none of the Nazis really needed to. They
all knew who Hitler was and what he stood for. It is
commonly asserted, however, that had the leaders of
other countries read Hitler's book, they might have
stopped him before he plunged the world into war.

There was, understandably, little interest in *Mein
Kampf* outside of Germany until Hitler came to power
in 1933. But then, Hitler attempted to disguise the full
extent of his ambitions by allowing only abridged edi-
tions to be published abroad. Much was omitted, including his plans to destroy the world's democracies. Most
of the anti-Jewish diatribes were left in, Hitler apparently
believing these would not have an adverse effect on general world opinion.

At least one world leader was not misled by the
abridged edition. The copy which belonged to Franklin
Roosevelt is preserved in the library of his Hyde Park
home. On its flyleaf, President Roosevelt wrote this:

The White House—1933—This translation is so
expurgated as to give a wholly false view of what

Hitler is and says—the German original would make a different story.

The British were equally well informed. Their Embassy in Berlin supplied them with detailed descriptions of the full-length version. These and other digests were circulated throughout the government by the Foreign Office and studied carefully.

Mein Kampf was not ignored. The problem seems to have been that few people could bring themselves to believe Hitler would really attempt what he threatened. He was, after all, a politician and politicians must anchor themselves in reality or disappear. Only a savage lunatic would actually try to conquer the world.

In 1939, British and American publishers issued complete translations of *Mein Kampf* without Hitler's approval. All profits were donated to charity. The Book of the Month Club offered it as a main selection, but had to downgrade it to "alternate" because of lack of subscriber interest. A number of short pamphlets and digests highlighting *Mein Kampf*'s true nature did achieve sales in the hundreds of thousands, including one prepared by Alan Cranston, who later became the senior Senator from California. (The American publishers of *Mein Kampf* sued Cranston's publishers over copyright infringement. This became the basis for an enduring popular legend that Cranston was sued by Hitler.)

Hitler made any number of predictions in *Mein Kampf*. Some were wildly wrong; for example, he did say that ultimately Japan and the United States would go to war but he also asserted that Britain would be Japan's principal ally in this struggle.

Sometimes he was right, and ignored his own warning at immense cost. He said Germany must never ally herself with the Soviet Union for that would inevitably unleash a war that would result in "the end of Germany."

More than a decade later, in August, 1939, he concluded an alliance with the Soviet Union that allowed Germany to seize half of Poland (and the Soviets to take the other half). And that, of course, triggered the Second World War.

FOUR

Hitler's Names and Titles

. . . Schicklgruber seemed to him so uncouth, so boorish, apart from being so clumsy and impractical.

—AUGUST KUBIZEK, BOYHOOD
FRIEND OF HITLER

Because Hitler's career depended to such a great degree on the image he projected, an awkward name would have been a severe handicap. Even the most obedient and adoring of Nazis might have had difficulty saluting his Fuehrer with a crisp "Heil Schicklgruber!"

Journalists in Austria, in the years when Hitler was still only threatening to annex that country, were the first to claim Hitler's real name was Schicklgruber. They meant to mock him, and to suggest he was illegitimate. In fact, Hitler was born Hitler, but the truth about Schicklgruber is significant.

Schicklgruber was his grandmother's name, and she *was* unmarried when her son Alois was born; thus, Hitler's father was named Alois Schiklgruber. It was not until he was thirty-nine years old that he appeared at the local church and asked that his name be changed in the birth register. He claimed that his father was one Johann Georg Hiedler.

Despite the fact that Hiedler had been dead for twenty years, Alois's claim was accepted and Schicklgruber became Hiedler—which can be spelled several ways, including the form Alois chose and Adolf made notorious.

Alois's motive for the name change is obscure; evidence suggests a maneuver to obtain a legacy.

Because the identity of Alois's father—Hitler's grandfather—cannot be established, many myths have flourished, including the one which asserts that Hitler was part Jewish. There is no evidence to substantiate this, and much to discredit it.

The significant point is simple. Hitler did not know who his grandfather was and yet (or perhaps because of this uncertainty, according to historians who have investigated his psychology), a crackpot theory about genetic purity became the basis of Nazi philosophy. After Hitler came to power, a citizen who wished to prove he was "uncontaminated" by non-German (most particularly, Jewish) blood, had to be able to trace his lineage at least through his grandparents, and this Hitler himself could not do.

Adolf

Hitler liked to point out that his first name was a contraction of two old German words, "Altha" and "Wolfa," which taken together mean Noble Wolf.

"Herr Wolf" was the name he chose when it was necessary for him to travel in secrecy in the early days of Nazi Party intriguing. When he telephoned Winnifred

Wagner, the great composer's daughter-in-law and an important early supporter, he identified himself with a coy "Conductor Wolf calling." Another doting dowager addressed him as "my little wolfie."

In later years, after he had pitched the world into war, he gave many of his field headquarters melodramatic wolf designations—Wolf's Glen, Wolf's Lair, Were-wolf.

Finally, it is reliably reported that Hitler's self-identification with wolves went so far that in moments of distraction he would absentmindedly whistle a favorite tune, "Who's Afraid of the Big Bad Wolf?"

Ade

In the early days, Hitler's associates often addressed him with nicknames such as "Ade," "Adi" and "Ahi." In conversation, many used the familiar second person pronoun, "du," rather than the more formal "sie."

Behind his back, some Nazis referred to him as "the Manitou." "Manitou" is an American Indian term for a kind of haunting spirit, often malevolent.

Fuehrer

"Fuehrer" means Leader. In July, 1921, Hitler quit the Nazi Party in a dispute over policy, saying he would return only if he were acknowledged as the Party's Leader without question. Since it was Hitler's single-minded energy and oratorical power which had earned the obscure Party any attention at all, the members agreed to his demand and he was hailed as the Fuehrer.

People closely associated with him continued to use nicknames and address him familiarly. Throughout his career members of his entourage usually referred to him as "der Chef," (the Chief).

As his power grew, he sought ways to further glorify himself. Late in 1931, Party members were officially directed henceforth to address him always and as nothing less than, "mein Fuehrer."

On January 30, 1933, Hitler acquired a new and very significant title when President Hindenburg appointed him Chancellor of Germany. (The President was the Chief of State, while the Chancellor ran the government.) A year and a half later, when Hindenburg died (of natural causes), Hitler eliminated the title of President, assumed the powers of the office, and created a new government title—Fuehrer and Reich Chancellor. (Later, Hitler said, "Anyone at all can be made a president, but it's not possible to give the title of 'Fuehrer' to a nobody.")

At the end of June 1934, Hitler secured his power with a brief but thorough wave of murders known as the Blood Purge. Its victims included opponents outside the Party but it was principally directed against a Nazi faction making demands he found inconvenient. The most prominent member of this faction was Ernst Roehm, leader of the brown shirt Storm Troopers and formerly a close Hitler associate.

After these murders, no one used the familiar "du" in addressing Hitler.

Grofaz

In the wake of the conquest of France in June 1940, Hitler's sycophantic underlings competed in their gushing compliments. Foremost among these was his Chief of Staff, Field Marshal Keitel, who dubbed Hitler "Grosster Feldherr aller Zeiten" (Greatest Commander of All Time)—commonly contracted to "Grofaz." Thereafter, Hitler gurgled with pleasure when he was thus addressed or when the term was skillfully dropped within earshot.

In 1942, Hitler assumed one more title, "Oberster Gerichsher," which means Supreme Judge. His word was now quite literally the law. This of course only formalized a situation which had prevailed for years.

By 1943, it was becoming increasingly clear to everyone that the Nazi cause was doomed, or at least Hitler was. An English journalist noted that Propaganda Minister Goebbels wasn't using the word Fuehrer nearly as much as he once had in his articles and speeches. Instead, the term "Fuehrung" often appeared. "Fuehrung" means the Leadership, of which the Leader is only a part. Was Goebbels preparing the public for something? After the war, it was learned that when complaining to his inner circle about the course of the war, Goebbels often muttered, "If I were the Fuehrer . . ."

Fortunately for Goebbels, no one seems to have mentioned these mutterings to Hitler. As for the public use of Fuehrung, Hitler was getting to the point where he no longer wanted to take responsibility for what was happening. Routinely, he complained that his Generals were letting him down, not following his orders, betraying him. Like the Nazis who would survive the war, he was already ducking the blame.

In the end, Goebbels apparently decided there was no Fuehrer, no Leader, but Adolf Hitler. Within hours after Hitler's suicide, Goebbels killed himself, as did his wife. Before this final act, which they regarded as proving their devotion to their Fuehrer, this monstrous couple poisoned their children.

FIVE
The Nazi Swastika

*A new age of magic interpretation of the world
is coming.*

—HITLER

Hitler imagined himself a great originator, a genius, but when the Nazis were just getting started and needed their own slogans and symbols, he seemed incapable of actually creating anything. He was, however, good at borrowing and adapting. Some of his sources are surprising.

Sieg Heil!

... means "Hail Victory!" An essential element of the huge Nazi rallies was the repeated, coordinated shouting of phrases like "Sieg Heil" and "Heil Hitler." Hitler got the idea for this from an old American custom.

His friend Ernst Hanfstaengl, although German, had been sent by his parents to study at Harvard. He also happened to be a skilled amateur pianist, and Hitler frequently had him play the Wagner melodies he found relaxing and inspiring. One night, sometime in the early

1920s, Hanfstaengl departed from the usual repertoire with a sampling of music Hitler had never heard before—the marches used at halftime in American football games. Hanfstaengl described college cheerleading and "the deliberate whipping up of hysterical enthusiasm." He told Hitler about the thousands of spectators being led in roars of, "Harvard, Harvard, Harvard, rah, rah, rah!" and about "the hypnotic effect of this sort of thing."

Hitler was wildly enthusiastic. "That is it, Hanfstaengl, that is what we need for the movement, marvelous." And as he said this, Hitler "pranced up and down the room like a drum majorette."

Hanfstaengl concludes his account of this extraordinary episode by saying, " . . . 'Rah, rah, rah!' became 'Sieg Heil, Sieg Heil!'—that is the origin of it and I suppose I must take my share of the blame."

Heil Hitler

At one time, using "Heil" (Hail) as a greeting was completely free of sinister connotation. Merely an enthusiastic form of "Hello," it was a customary salutation in Austria and Bavarian Germany, where the Nazi Party got started.

In the Party's early days, Nazis commonly used the Heil greeting among themselves, as in "Heil Hanfstaengl" or "Heil Ludecke." In time, the phrase "Heil Hitler" became a kind of insider's password by which Nazis made themselves known to one another. Ultimately, as part of establishing an exalted status for Hitler, it was ruled improper for anyone but him to be addressed with "Heil."

After the Nazis came to power, "Heil Hitler" was designated the official "German greeting," to be used by all
citizens in all communications, verbal and written. This
directive was widely obeyed, usually with genuine enthusiasm.

Hitler Salute

The rigidly outstretched right arm salute was copied
from the Italian Fascists of Benito Mussolini, who was
firmly in power by the end of 1922, when Hitler still
only dreamt of ruling Germany. Indeed, for years, Hitler
was routinely identified in American and English newspapers as the German Mussolini.

Hitler bragged that he could hold the salute far longer
than any of his subordinates and at ceremonies and re-
views did exhibit a remarkable endurance. Contemporary legend ascribed this to a collapsible spring support
under his jacket sleeve.

It is certain that it was highly dangerous for bystand-
ers *not* to give the Nazi salute when Hitler's Storm
Troopers paraded through a city's streets. The marchers
would break ranks and attack any who thus failed to
show their respect, often beating them senseless. This
happened so commonly that American tourists were
warned by the American Ambassador to either give the
salute or get off the street when they saw a parade coming.

Nazi

Apocryphal tales surround the word, "Nazi"; the truth is simple and straightforward.

The group Hitler joined in late 1919 was called the German Workers' Party. Four months later, to show its affinity with other radical nationalist organizations, the group added a designation used by many of them—National Socialist. Thus, the still small organization acquired its long name—National Socialist German Workers' Party.

Hitler wanted to dump all this and use the simpler "Social Revolutionary Party" but he was not yet in control. By the time he was, he was stuck with the unwieldy name.

He and fellow members called themselves National Socialists; "Nazi" was a common and not inherently derogatory contraction of this.

However, American reporters broadcasting from Germany before the war were ordered to drop the term and to always employ "National Socialist" instead. The Germans had come to the conclusion that as a word, Nazi had "a bad sound" in America and that getting rid of it would improve their image.

Third Reich

Hitler's regime is often referred to as the Third Reich, a term vigorously promoted by Propaganda Minister Goebbels. "Reich" means "Empire." The first Reich was the Holy Roman Empire of the Middle Ages; the second, the one established by Bismarck and ended by Germany's defeat in 1918.

Hitler himself rarely referred to his rule as the Third Reich, and at the beginning of World War II actually outlawed its use. He spoke simply of the Reich, as though there had never been another.

Nazi propaganda also described the regime as the Thousand Year Reich. This term has a particularly lethal history. In June 1934, a year and a half after becoming Chancellor of Germany, Hitler ordered the wave of assassinations and executions called the Blood Purge, directed principally at rivals within the Party. He excused these murders by saying his rivals had been plotting revolution, and promised there would be no further upheavals in Germany for a thousand years. In fact, of course, his Reich lasted little more than twelve years.

The Swastika

A tremendous amount of nonsense has been written about the purported occult power of the emblem the Nazis adopted as their own—the swastika. This sort of thing pleased Hitler very much because he knew people were awed by mystery, and swayed by it.

In fact, the swastika is an ancient symbol, most probably meant to represent the sun wheeling across the sky. It first appeared in ancient India, is found in cultures throughout the world, and—until the Nazis got hold of it—was regarded for thousands of years as a symbol of good fortune. (In some mythologies, a swastika whose arms point to the left instead of the right signifies darkness and evil.)

Hitler may have first seen a swastika (arms pointing right) at the age of seven, while taking singing lessons in a church in the town of Lambach. The bishop of Lambach's coat of arms included a swastika, and one was carved above the pulpit.

August Kubizek, his boyhood friend, reports that Hitler again encountered the ancient symbol while reading about Nordic gods and early German tribes and thought it important. "Adolf said at that time that the German people needed a symbol which would represent the basic concept of Germandom."

After the First World War, Hitler toyed briefly with the idea of writing a "monumental history" of mankind. He scribbled a brief outline for this and when he sketched the design for a cover, he included a swastika flag.

However, the swastika was not a great Hitler discovery. It had been used for years by many of the radical right-wing groups which flourished throughout Germany and Austria. The Nazis were among the last to pick it up but then Hitler did make every effort to employ it to maximum effect, lavishing his personal attention on designing the badges, flags, standards and armbands featuring it. He insisted it always be a black swastika set in a white circle and—most importantly—the background must always be red. That was the color that captured people's attention, he said, adding this was something he had learned from the Socialists.

In time, the swastika and Nazism were synonymous. On March 12, 1933, six weeks after he became Chancellor, Hitler announced that henceforth whenever the German flag was displayed, the swastika flag of the Nazi Party would fly alongside it.

Finally, at the annual Party Rally in Nuremberg in

September 1935, he decreed that the swastika alone would represent both the Party and the nation. The one-party state was firmly established. (At the same time, the notorious "Nuremberg Laws" were promulgated, forbidding marriage between Jews and non-Jews, and depriving all German Jews of citizenship.)

SIX

Henry Ford's Nazi Medal

*Henry Ford—to Europeans, the incarnation of
wealth in its alluring bulk.*

—KURT LUDECKE, HITLER AIDE

In 1937, Hitler created a special new medal—the Cross
of the German Eagle Order—for foreign friends of the
Reich. The first American to whom it was awarded was
Henry Ford.

Consisting of a Maltese cross bracketed with four eagles and four swastikas, it was clearly a Nazi medal and
although its presentation to Ford was ostensibly only to
honor him on his seventy-fifth birthday, it may have really been acknowledgment for past services rendered to
the Nazi cause.

The connection between Hitler and Ford went back at
least fifteen years. In 1922, a reporter visiting Nazi headquarters in Munich noted that a large portrait of Ford
hung on the wall beside Hitler's desk.

Without question, Ford and Hitler had something in
common, at least at that time. They both hated Jews.
Ford had bought an American newspaper, the Dearborn
Independent, and used it to publish a long series of ar-

ticles which claimed that for centuries Jews had been systematically conspiring to destroy Christian civilization. Their crimes, Ford insisted, included starting the First World War.

The Dearborn *Independent* was a small town paper when Ford bought it but achieved a nationwide circulation of nearly 750,000 a week, in large part because Ford dealerships throughout the country were required to sell it.

Eventually, the *Independent*'s anti-Semitic articles were collected and published under the title, *The International Jew*. The German translation became a best-seller.

Hitler was enthusiastic about *The International Jew*, had copies prominently displayed at Nazi headquarters, and ultimately ordered it translated into a dozen other languages and distributed throughout the world.

There may have been an even more sinister connection between Ford and Hitler. Rumors circulated in the early 1920s that Ford was pouring money into the Nazi Party; the story was plausible enough for the senior American Vice Consul in Munich to visit Hitler in person and ask about it.

Hitler denied the rumor but his words suggested he was hopeful. He said, "Mr. Ford's organization has so far made no money contributions to our Party."

It was soon clear that had contributions been uncovered, the United States would have been involved in a serious international incident. About eight months after the Vice Consul's visit, Hitler attempted the violent overthrow of the government which became known as the "Beer Hall Putsch." If Ford had been financing Hitler, he would have been financing revolution.

It must be said that despite renewed assertions in the wake of the uprising—and a U.S. Congressional investigation—no concrete evidence was ever found proving that Hitler had received money from Ford. In 1927, Ford professed a change of heart and disavowed his anti-Semitism.

However, eleven years later, in April 1938 and well into the rapid Nazi rearmament, when Hitler asked him to build a truck and automobile assembly plant in Berlin, Ford agreed. Construction was soon under way, and in July Ford was awarded his swastika-studded Cross of the German Eagle Order.

In October of that year, another famous American received the Cross—Charles Lindbergh. It wasn't anti-Semitism or industrial support that endeared Lindbergh to Hitler, but a convergence of views on American foreign policy and Nazism. Lindbergh said repeatedly and publicly that the United States ought to stay out of European affairs, by which he meant the United States ought not to oppose Hitler.

He said any such intervention would be doomed because Germany's air power made her unbeatable, and in any event he evidently didn't think Hitler was evil and dangerous because he argued that Nazism might well be superior to democracy as a form of government.

Hitler could not have invented a more perfect propagandist.

Undoubtedly, neither Ford nor Lindbergh knew what Hitler really thought of the medal he gave them, the Cross of the German Eagle Order. In a private conversation with his cronies, he made a remark that was an extraordinary combination of nationalistic arrogance and penny-pinching. He said he had created the special medal so no purely German decoration would be defiled by being given to a foreigner. Also, "this new decoration will be a lot cheaper than the gold or silver cigarette cases which the Reich was formerly wont to present to foreigners."

In his heart, Hitler almost always had contempt for those who served him.

SEVEN

The Fuehrer's Volkswagen

The Volkswagen—and I think our war experiences justify us in saying so—is the car of the future.

—HITLER

A year after taking power, Hitler announced at the Berlin Auto Show of 1934 that he would do for Germany what Henry Ford had done for America—create a mass-produced car anyone could afford. The result was the Volkswagen beetle, the biggest selling car of all time.

Hitler had always been fascinated by automobiles, although he never learned to drive one. He used chauffeurs, claiming he dared not drive because of his political prominence. In the event of an accident, he said, the blame would inevitably fall on him. Perhaps this was his sole motive but it is quite likely that he refused to attempt driving for the same reason he rarely undertook anything new. Learning to drive would have meant a period of awkwardness and failure. Hitler believed a man who intended to rule the world should never be seen falling short in any respect. He must appear infallible, always and at everything.

Hitler's interest in cars was so great as to be one of the few things which could distract him from his political career. In the years when he was campaigning for power, he traveled incessantly throughout Germany, speaking at rallies and meetings; but sometimes, when he arrived in a town he had not been in before, he failed to show up for the scheduled appearance. The aides who went looking for him did not bother with bars or brothels. They knew they would find him browsing at the local automobile dealer's showroom.

At first he could afford only used cars but as his financing improved, Hitler moved up to new cars—always Mercedes, and always powerful. On one occasion, in Nuremberg, when he was bragging about his latest 200 h.p. acquisition, two colleagues challenged him, claiming that on ordinary roads, with curves and traffic, all that power would give him no advantage. Hitler took the dare and granted the two a fifteen-minute head start on the road back to Munich.

They raced off but soon realized Hitler was catching up, so when they got to the next town they turned off the road and hid behind a church. The trick worked. Hitler roared by and kept going. After he had cleared the town, the challengers got back on the road and, keeping out of sight, trailed him as he spent the rest of the day in a frustrated attempt to pass them. Later, in Munich, when they confessed what they had done, he stalked off in anger.

The Beetle Is Born

Although Volkswagens became so closely associated with him as to be popularly dubbed "Baby Hitlers" by

Germans, the idea of producing an automobile the average German could afford did not originate with Hitler. Ferdinand Porsche, famous for his high performance cars, had been developing a "people's car" (volkswagen) for some time when he was summoned for a meeting with the Fuehrer in May 1934.

Hitler looked over Porsche's designs and ordered changes, directing the car be air-cooled and that it be a four-seater so it could serve as a family car. It was at this meeting that he also gave the VW its characteristic shape, and one of its most famous nicknames. For the sake of streamlining, he said it "should look like a beetle."

Because almost everything Hitler did was destructive and repulsive, it may seem inconsistent that he was capable of suggesting anything useful. He may have just gotten lucky on this. During the war, he decided that naval designers erred when they put propellers at the rear of ships. The Navy at the time had its hands full with, among other things, the Battle of the Atlantic and trying to supply the North African campaign, but Hitler ordered resources be devoted to the building of a ship with its screws along the side.

The project was a flop. Indeed, Hitler's ideas about science and technology—and his insistence in exerting his will in these areas—proved to be a substantial handicap in the development of advanced weapons which might have changed the outcome of the war (see chapter 28, "Hitler's Atomic Bomb").

Although Hitler did have some good ideas about the Volkswagen, the official name he chose was not one of them. Porsche wanted "Volkswagen" but Hitler insisted on "KdF-Wagen." KdF was a contraction of the German words meaning Strength Through Joy.

The Strength Through Joy program provided vacations, recreational facilities and other amenities that were supposed to make life beautiful for German workers and their families. The program achieved some popularity but many Germans referred to it by another phrase the initials of which are also KdF—*Kotz durchs Fenster*—which means Vomit Through the Window.

At some point, Hitler gave up and began using "Volkswagen" himself.

Handmade Models Only

The first, hand-built Volkswagens were shown in 1938, four years after Hitler announced the program, but they were not available to the public.

Asked when they would be, the German Press Attache in Washington joked that the VW ought to be called "Christ" because "everyone talks about Him without having seen Him."

To get the Volkswagen into mass production, the Nazis came up with a unique twist on time-payment. Instead of the customer making a down payment, getting the car, and then paying it off, Germans were expected to pay the full price in advance and thus underwrite the production. People who elected to do this were given a booklet into which they were to paste stamps they received in return for a weekly 5-mark payment. After four years and eleven months of this, they would have paid the full sales price of 990 marks (plus 200 marks for insurance), and the car would be theirs. A thousand marks was roughly the equivalent of $400.

Ultimately, more than three hundred thousand Germans subscribed for the new car. Some, no doubt, subscribed with optimism; others were only obeying the unwritten rules of life in a totalitarian state.

The total number of Volkswagen cars actually produced before the war barely exceeded two hundred, and these were given to top Nazi officials, including Hitler. His was kept at his mountain estate near Berchtesgaden because it was particularly well suited to the steep, narrow roads.

It was Hitler's habit each day to walk from the Berghof, his chalet, to a small tea house nearby. When it was time to return to the Berghof, he often called for his chauffeur and his Volkswagen. (It was grayish-blue in color, as were all the VWs.)

As Hitler pursued his bellicose foreign policy, the German public began to suspect the Volkswagen factory might not be making what the customers were paying for. A new joke circulated: a worker at the VW plant decided he would get a car for himself by sneaking out the parts and assembling them at home. Imagine his surprise, went the story, when he was done and found the finished product was not a family car, but a motorized gun carrier.

By the time the main Volkswagen plant at Wolfsburg was fully operational, there was no question of its producing cars for civilians. Instead, the plant began turning out the German equivalent of the Jeep, called the Kubelwagen ("Bucket Car"). Years after the war, this model became a great commercial success, marketed in the U.S. as "The Thing." During the war the factory also produced a version of the Kubelwagen called the Schwimmwagen, for amphibious operations. It had a sealed, waterproof body and a retractable propeller (in the rear).

The factory also produced airplane parts and at one point was assembling sixty V-1 "buzz bombs" a day. The V-1, the first of Hitler's "Vengeance Weapons," was the pilotless robot jet used against London.

A series of Allied bombing raids succeeded in putting the VW factory almost completely out of operation by August 1944. It was only after the war that bomb disposal experts discovered how close one particular bomb had come to putting an end to the Volkswagen forever. It had scored a direct hit, falling right between the two great turbines which powered the factory. An explosion would have destroyed them and the Volkswagen car would probably have become one of the "might have beens" of history. But there was no explosion. The direct hit had been a dud.

By the summer of 1945, the plant was back in production, assembling a small number of Kubelwagens for the occupying British. At the very end of the year, the production of VW Beetles began. By March 1946, a thousand cars a month were coming off the assembly line.

The original three hundred thousand subscribers never got anything for their money, but by 1948, the VW was finally being offered through a regular dealership network.

By the time production of the basic model was discontinued in the middle of 1985, more than twenty million had been sold . . . none of them called KdF-Wagens, but all of them shaped like beetles.

EIGHT

Backstage Hitler

Agitation, moral indignation, sympathy, shock, sincerity, condolence, reverence—he had a posture for everything.

—ERNST VON WEISZACKER,
NAZI DIPLOMAT

Hitler wanted to be seen as impulsive, emotional, inspired. In fact, he was a cool manipulator who carefully planned for maximum effect. He even had himself photographed after buying new clothes so he could study his appearance from all angles. If the result was unsatisfactory, the new clothes were discarded.

When Hitler decided to change the style of his military hat, someone had an ingenious idea which spared him the modeling sessions. A wax sculpture of his head was made and sent to the hat factory, where the various styles were placed on it and photographed. But when the pictures were delivered to Hitler, he suspected a plot.

There was nothing wrong with the hats. It was the wax head; the mustache on it was too broad—rather like Stalin's, in fact—and Hitler suspected he was being insulted.

The thorough investigation which was immediately undertaken failed to establish that anyone had intentionally tried to belittle the Fuehrer by suggesting a similarity with the Soviet dictator.

Rehearsing

Before an important meeting with someone he was to see for the first time, Hitler often had an associate meet the other party in advance and make an assessment so he could prepare himself accordingly. This was not a matter of organizing arguments or facts and figures, but of deciding which Hitler *persona* to present—which role to play.

The gist of one of these rehearsals has been preserved. In this particular case, Rudolf Hess was the advance scout. Hitler asks if the man he is to meet "can be used." Hess replies that he can. Hitler then asks, "What does he expect?"

Hess: Authority, of course. You can speak
        at length. Your will is unshakable.
        You give laws to the age.
Hitler: Then I'll speak with the firm voice,
        without yelling?
Hess: Of course.

Having decided that the appropriate impression for this interview ought to be firmness but not fanaticism, Hitler then practices for several minutes until he finds just the right style and tone. Finally, he concludes his conference with Hess by saying, "Good, now I think we have it." The meeting can now be scheduled.

Carpet Chewing

Hitler commonly sucked his fingers and chewed his nails, habits he was careful to refrain from in public. He was, however, famous for a behavior in which he never indulged.

Even Nazis sometimes referred to him as the "teppichfresser," which means "carpet chewer," because a common rumor had him throwing himself to the floor and chewing on the carpet during his famous rages. There is no recorded instance of Hitler ever actually doing this, perhaps because it would have been going too far. Indeed, Hitler was in complete control of himself most of the time. Many of the famous Hitler tantrums were just part of the act.

Sometimes, of course, they were deeply genuine, and there was no way of telling which of the rages were assumed and which were authentic. They were always impressive. Even associates of long standing were intimidated as Hitler stamped his feet and pounded his fists on tables and walls. Literally foaming at the mouth, he would roar: "I won't have it! Get rid of them all! Traitors!" and so forth. His eyes became fixed, his face reddened and darkened to purple, a large blue vein running down his forehead bulged.

It was as much the unpredictable onset of these rages as their passion that threw everyone into helpless confusion. And of course for hours or days afterward, there was the tension, the waiting to learn whether this particular storm would pass off without incident or had been the prelude to new terror and murder.

Preparing a Speech

In the early days, until about 1930, Hitler prepared for a speech by scribbling out key words and phrases on small sheets of paper. He generally used between ten and twelve of these, with no more than fifteen or twenty words to a sheet. A typical effort began with the words, "Jewish domination and starvation of the nation" and ended with "Germany will be free notwithstanding." The notes in between included such promptings as "Want-Misery-Scarcity-Famine," "The Jew as fission fungus" and of course, "the world under one master."

As the Party became more affluent and able to afford secretarial staff, Hitler changed his procedure and began dictating his speeches to typists, often working without any notes at all. Teams of typists had to be kept ready on round-the-clock standby as he brooded and mulled until the last possible moment. Then, not one but two of the typists were summoned—nothing must interrupt the Fuehrer as he spewed forth words in a session that usually lasted for hours.

Oratorical Poses

In the early 1920s, Hitler may or may not have taken lessons in public speaking from a sometime actor, sometime astrologer who went by the name of Erik Jan Hanussen (and whose real name was Herschel Steinschneider). The facts are obscure. It is certain, though, that in 1925 Hitler posed for a remarkable set of photographs as part of perfecting his overall oratorical style.

There are no crowds in these pictures, no swastika banners or uniforms—just Hitler, in an ordinary suit against a plain background in a series of oratorical poses. The photos allowed him to study his appearance as he practiced the emphatic gestures: one depicts the upraised fist; another, the admonitory pointing finger; a third, the openhanded appeal to reason. Clearly, Hitler understood oratory as melodramatic theater.

Last Minute Preparations

He manipulated his audience in every way that he could. During the days when he was still speaking to comparatively small crowds, building popular support on his way to the seizure of power, he sent advance scouts to the hall in the hours before he was scheduled to appear. These scouts supplied a steady stream of telephone reports: the size of the audience . . . were people still arriving . . . what was the overall mood of the crowd, would there be any opposition or argument?

Hitler was always preceded by other speakers and as each prepared to take the platform, Hitler telephoned last minute instructions on how he wanted the crowd worked up—whether they were to be moved toward good humor or rage.

Hitler made one last preparation before finally setting out for the hall himself—pep pills. About fifteen minutes before speaking, Hitler took two Kola-Dallmann tablets, a stimulant compounded of cola, caffeine and sugar.

Later, particularly during the war years, he would become increasingly dependent on a wide variety of drugs (see chapter 13, "Hitler the Hypochondriac"). While he was still on the way to power, though, the Kola-Dallmann tablets sufficed to provide just the kick he needed as he approached the platform and his audience.

NINE

Hitler Speaks

Hitler's voice sounds *tremendously sincere and convincing.*

—WILLIAM SHIRER
DIARY ENTRY, MAY 1935

Hitler's voice was a powerful instrument; when enraged about one thing or another, his shouting could rattle windows in their frames.

He could erupt at any time. On one occasion, during dinner at an acquaintance's home, he was sitting quietly enough until someone was so unwise as to say something in defense of Jews. (This was well before Hitler was in power. After that, no one would have dared make such a remark.) Hitler immediately launched into a tirade, pushing back his chair and speaking with such force that a child sleeping in another room woke and began to cry. This went on for more than half an hour.

When he was finally finished, Hitler bowed to his hostess, kissed her hand, and left without further ado. The guest who reports all this also notes that Hitler's remarks were "quite witty."

He did have an extraordinary verbal range. When he

45

wished to impress a visitor with his sweet gentility, he spoke with his "cooing voice," the voice of the dove, and the visitor came away thinking he had been granted a privileged insight. Surely, he thought, he had met the real Hitler, a reasonable man with no intention of carrying out the threats he made in public.

The War Voice

Hitler could do more with his voice than just speak. He sometimes entertained his intimates with vocal impressions of automobiles and other kinds of machinery, but his favorite subject was warfare. He was able to accurately mimic the sound of machine-gun fire, or a particular kind of howitzer, or the roar and screech of vast artillery barrages.

Indeed, war had helped shape his voice. Serving as a foot soldier in the First World War (see chapter 10, "Hitler in Combat"), he had been caught in a gas attack which temporarily blinded him and permanently damaged his throat, leaving his voice hoarse and rasping.

He had to learn to speak again, and this process helped confirm an idea that was to become a central Hitler concept—that in some real sense, he *was* Germany. His voice had nearly been destroyed by the war, but through his will it had become stronger than ever. And so, he said, the German nation would recover from its defeat and—through him—revenge itself upon the world.

The Orator

One of Hitler's schoolteachers later claimed he had witnessed his young pupil talking to trees. Perhaps this was because the trees did not talk back. Hitler was never much interested in conversation. By the time he was a teenager he was confirmed in his habit of talking on and on like a phonograph record once a favorite topic got him started. Oratory became an essential part of his ordinary life.

When he entered into his political career after the First World War, his oratorical ease allowed him to automatically employ the language of the common citizen rather than the stilted, abstract imagery of conventional German political speakers. When he talked of economic difficulties, for example, he used the terms and phrases housewives used.

He made his audience think he was their man.

The Performance

Observers, even when they had taken notes, often found it impossible to summarize a Hitler speech. Although Hitler had mapped its course in advance, there was little logic to the structure, and he compounded the incoherence by digressing into prolix tangents as they occurred to him. His audiences did not care. This orator persuaded not with reason but with emotion. His speeches were performances.

The performances began with music. As Hitler entered the hall or stadium where he would be speaking, it was always to the accompaniment of the music he had adopted as his personal motif—a banging, swinging military tune called the "Badenweiler March."

When he took the podium and started to speak, his manner was tentative, for he was still gauging the exact emotional climate of his audience, attuning himself like a nightclub performer.

He usually opened with the historical background of the issue at hand, and no matter the specifics of this review, the theme was almost always the same. An outrage had been committed against the German nation, the German people. The perpetrator was usually the Jews, although sometimes it was the Capitalists, or the Communists, or the Poles, or President Roosevelt.

Soon Hitler was well into the pace of his speech, moving briskly, confidently. Anger was always an important component of his style, expressed in every conceivable form—scorn, ridicule, threats, insults. Crude humor was also abundant in vulgar jokes, mockery, exaggerated impersonations of the enemy.

The audience was not passive through all this. Far from it. They were encouraged—expected—to participate with frequent applause, laughter and shouts of agreement. Even members of the Reichstag, the rubber stamp legislature, played "hiss the villain" when Hitler mentioned an arch fiend like Winston Churchill. Churchill's name was greeted with what the official German news agency reported as "catcalls and cries of 'Pfui'."

Always, near the end, there was a distinct shift in the mood of a speech, toward the rhapsodic. Hitler's outspread hands rose high and he looked toward Heaven, transported by exaltation. He was not merely speaking; he was acting out a promise—the coming triumph and redemption of the German people, usually through an act of vengeance.

Seduction

Hitler's performances contained an undeniably erotic element. A contemporary witness saw the Fuehrer as an insignificant little man stiffened by his own words as a hose is stiffened by its stream of water. The conclusions of his speeches are described as orgasmic. In one instance, he beamed at the audience and said, "Aren't you as enthralled by me as I am with you?"

It was not uncommon for women to swoon during a Hitler speech. When discussing propaganda theory, Hitler described the public in general as a feminine mass waiting to be conquered, overwhelmed. This may really have been his perception, and the idea was certainly useful to Germans after 1945. They had been seduced, they said, by Hitler's hypnotic influence. Contemporary accounts say something else. They suggest that in fact Hitler was a kind of human radio, picking up a signal from his audience and, with little modulation, amplifying it. One Hitler associate, Otto Strasser, saw him as a kind of loudspeaker "proclaiming the most secret desires, the least admissible instincts, the suffering and personal revolts of a whole nation."

Perhaps the most frightening thing about Hitler's career is not that he was successful at imposing himself on general public opinion but that he was so good at representing it.

TEN

Hitler in Combat

*Then a bullet tore off my right sleeve but by a
miracle I was saved.*

—HITLER, 1915, IN A LETTER
HOME, DESCRIBING A
W.W.I EXPERIENCE

What a tantalizing vision—Hitler killed in the First
World War. Unfortunately, he not only survived
the fighting; he thrived on it. It offered him a fulfillment
he could find nowhere else, and it inspired some of his
most dangerous ideas.

Ironically, Hitler first came to the attention of military
authorities as a draft dodger. He was an Austrian, and
Austrian law required that he register for the draft when
he reached his twentieth birthday, in 1909. He failed to
do this and it is thought by many historians that his need
to elude the authorities accounts for his frequent changes
of address after this date.

A popular legend has him spending some months in
England during this period, visiting his brother-in-law
(see chapter 13, "William Patrick Hitler"). This story,
though intriguing, has been discredited by historians

who have painstakingly tracked Hitler's actual whereabouts through his wandering years.

In 1913, he left Austria altogether and for the first
time in his life entered Germany. The Austrians tracked
him down in Munich and in February 1914, had him
returned. It soon developed, though, that his efforts at
evasion had been unnecessary. He failed the physical.
Judged too weak for military service, he was allowed to
return to Munich.

A German Soldier

Because Austria (actually, the Austro-Hungarian Empire)
was comprised of a variety of nationalities, Hitler regarded it as a mongrel nation. He considered himself a
German and, as it turned out, was more than willing to
fight for Germany.

When the Great War erupted in 1914, people on both
sides thought the fighting would be short and glorious,
but the prospect generated a special enthusiasm in Hitler.
By chance, his reaction was captured in an extraordinary
photograph. The picture is of a huge crowd assembled
to hear patriotic speeches the day Germany declared war
on Russia. Hitler was only an anonymous figure in this
vast throng, but with the aid of a magnifying glass his
face can be seen. It is transfigured by wild excitement,
joy.

(The photograph was taken by Heinrich Hoffmann,
who later became Hitler's personal photographer. Rem-
iniscing as to where each had been on that historic day
quickly led to the realization that Hitler had been in the
crowd Hoffmann was shooting.)

Almost immediately after the war began, Hitler joined a German unit. One of his fellow enlistees noticed something curious about him when rifles were issued. Hitler, he said, regarded his weapon "with the delight that a woman looks at her jewelry."

Within two months Hitler was under fire at the front, serving first as an ordinary soldier, then as a dispatch runner. Whereas most soldiers quickly grew to detest life at the front, Hitler enjoyed it. Another of his comrades later said, "We all cursed him and found him intolerable. There was this white crow among us that didn't go along with us when we damned this war to hell."

Perhaps the violence and danger slaked some twisted need in Hitler's soul. That is speculation. What is certain is that the war had a profound effect on his thinking.

He developed a profound admiration for the command structure of the German Imperial Army, and later imposed its essence on the Nazi Party and then on all German life. As he formulated it, the Fuehrerprinzip—the Leadership Principle—entailed absolute obedience by the lower ranks to the higher; the man on the top was the ultimate source of authority, without qualification or restriction. In Nazi Germany, the ultimate court, the fundamental law, was Hitler.

During the First World War, Hitler got little chance to exert authority over anyone because he was never promoted beyond the rank of lance corporal (private first class in the American system). His superiors judged that he lacked leadership potential. There was the matter of his not being much liked by his fellows, and he was certainly a crackpot. On one occasion he gave a lecture in the trenches about a new social order that would emerge after the war, but the audience he addressed was a row of clay figures he had made and set up on the parapet.

Hitler seems to have been content with things as they were. There is no record of his applying for advancement or complaining about the lack of it. Perhaps he had no interest in being a leader if he could not be *the* leader.

He did get something else from his Army experience besides the Fuehrerprinzip, something far more peculiar. Although he was wounded by shell splinters and debilitated by poison gas, he found enormous significance in all the incidents in which he was not wounded. There was the "miracle" of the bullet that only tore off his sleeve. On another occasion, he was sitting in a trench eating with his fellow soldiers when, he claimed, an inner voice impelled him to get up and move away. Moments later, a shell burst over the group, killing everyone.

Hitler was a habitual liar and it is entirely possible he invented stories about close calls. The fact remains, though, that he did survive four years on the Western front and was involved in approximately fifty major and minor battles. This survival confirmed his belief that what he called "Providence" had reserved a special destiny for him. In his post-war political career, there were a number of occasions when all seemed lost, but because he was confident of his Providential destiny he persevered in his effort to fulfill it, to make himself one of the most important men in history. His belief fueled his role as Messiah and helped him radiate that immense self-assurance many found so persuasive.

War Hero?

Hitler was awarded a number of decorations during the War, the most important of which was certainly the Iron Cross, First Class, which he received in 1918. This and only this was the medal he wore throughout the war he started twenty-one years later.

Hitler frequently reminisced about his First World War experiences, but said strangely little about how he had earned this important commendation. It was assumed by many, therefore, that he had not earned it but had managed to buy it or connive for it. Subsequent scholarship has cleared up the mystery.

He earned the medal fairly, risking his life carrying a vital message under particularly dangerous circumstances. What he was trying to cover up, it turns out, was nothing more or less than the fact that the medal had been recommended and pushed through by a company adjutant who was a Jew.

After the War

Hitler's Providential luck did not save him from the poison gas attack which sent him to the hospital in October 1918. He was still recuperating there less than a month later when the staggering news arrived that Germany had surrendered. The war was over. Hitler wept bitterly.

He remained in the Army, returned to Munich and there managed to keep clear of a chaotic sequence of Communist and anti-Communist uprisings and repressions.

After the Army finally reestablished order, the Generals resolved to keep a close eye on all political activity. Hitler became one of the men assigned to this duty.

On September 12, 1919, he was sent to observe a meeting of an obscure, very small group with an impressive name: the German Workers' Party. It had about fifty members.

Hitler sat through a speech he found boring, but the subsequent discussion was another matter. After someone advocated a position he disagreed with, he leapt to his feet and delivered a fiery impromptu reply.

This so impressed the membership that a few days later he was sent a postcard admitting him to the Party, even though he had not applied. After attending one more meeting he agreed to join. It was the very weakness of the group, its small size and lack of direction, that appealed to him. This was a group he could dominate. Here he could begin at the top and exercise the Fuehrerprinzip, with himself as the Fuehrer.

Six months later, he resigned from the Army.

ELEVEN

Hitler's Women

*Despite censorship, police, and denouncement,
Berlin society could not help but gossip.*

—ANDRE FRANCOIS-PONCET,
FRENCH AMBASSADOR TO
BERLIN

A number of factors gave rise to contemporary rumors
that Hitler was homosexual. There was his overall
manner—exaggerated and self-dramatizing, even when
he was not on the podium. And there was the way he
walked. Although it is not particularly apparent in newsreels, William Shirer noted in his diary that Hitler's gait
was "very ladylike . . . dainty little steps."

One of Hitler's closest associates, designated as the
Deputy Fuehrer, was Rudolf Hess, who was known in
homosexual circles as "Fraulein Hess" and "Fraulein
Anna."

Hess played a prominent role in Hitler's 1923 attempt
to overthrow the government. Because he was not sentenced until some time after Hitler, he remained in jail
for months after Hitler's release. Hitler was not happy
about this. He could not be happy, he said, until "mein

Rudi, mein Hesserl" was also free. "Hesserl" is fairly translated as "dear little Hess."

The homosexuality of another important Hitler associate, Ernst Roehm, is well established, and may have specially qualified him in Hitler's mind for his appointment as head of the Storm Troopers. The principal function of this army-like organization was beating up anyone who opposed the Nazis, and Hitler believed this was a job best undertaken by homosexuals. "No one with family responsibilities," he said, "is any good for street fighting."

There is no evidence, though, that Hitler ever had a homosexual relationship with Hess, Roehm or anyone else.

Purge

Four years after making Roehm head of the Storm Troopers, Hitler had him murdered in the Blood Purge, the massacre that consolidated his political position. When he made his explanations to the German public, he said one of the reasons he had acted was his shock at learning Roehm was homosexual and had been encouraging "degenerate" practices among the Storm Troopers.

Thereafter, the full power of the Nazi state was unleashed against homosexuals with a ferocity and thoroughness approaching that directed against Jews.

The OSS and Hitler's Perversion

Hitler may not have been homosexual but his relations with women were almost certainly peculiar.

In 1943, when the American Office of Strategic Services (OSS) commissioned a study of Hitler, it turned not to a historian or military expert, but to Dr. Walter Langer, a psychoanalyst.

After reviewing all the information available to him at that time, Langer concluded that Hitler achieved sexual satisfaction by having women urinate and defecate on him.

This kind of masochism is common enough to be well documented, and one of the things established about it is that even people who indulge in it are revolted by it. Langer, and others after him, believe Hitler's self-loathing was an essential motivating element in his character. They argue that he unconsciously denied his self-disgust by generalizing it and projecting it on to others (*e.g.* "filthy Jews"). His self-loathing may have also contributed to a powerful compensating drive, that insatiable desire for self-aggrandizement which propelled him throughout his maniacal career.

The Women

As far as is known, Hitler first fell in love at the age of sixteen, with a girl named Stefanie. He admired her from a distance, wrote her only one letter (which he did not sign) and never did get up the nerve to approach her or—so far as is known—any other woman during his adolescence.

In later years, persistent rumors circulated that sometime in his twenties, Hitler had contracted syphilis from a prostitute. The long-term effects of the disease, it was said, accounted for his subsequent "insane" behavior. In fact, the detailed medical evidence about Hitler that became available after the war proved he had never had syphilis (see chapter 13, "Hitler the Hypochondriac").

When he was in his thirties, he began systematically cultivating women, not for romance but for help with his morbid political career. Dubbed "the varicose vein squad" by his cronies, these were wealthy dowagers who found the impassioned young politician irresistible. He is reliably reported sitting at the feet of one of these women with his head on her bosom as she stroked his hair and murmured to her "little Wolfie."

"Little Wolfie" was in the habit of carrying a short whip most of the time, ostensibly to defend himself in the event of attack. Several of these whips were gifts from his older female admirers.

Of more significant historic consequence were the introductions these women supplied to a wide circle of influential and wealthy people. In this world, Hitler dropped his role as street orator–revolutionary, and—with occasional lapses—practiced instead his "reasonable man" act.

The doting dowagers would probably have been disconcerted to learn that Hitler's personal library included a collection of illustrated erotica (see chapter 17, "Hitler's Bookshelf") and that in later years he had pornographic movies specially made for him (chapter 18, "Hitler at the Movies").

In 1926, when he was thirty-seven years old, he fell in love, or least became infatuated, with a sixteen-year-old girl named Maria Reiter.

Their first date began normally enough. Chaperoned by her sister and one of his aides, they strolled in a forest with their dogs. Then, Hitler's dog disobeyed a command and Hitler demonstrated what he considered manly attractiveness by using his whip to beat the animal savagely.

Their walk concluded, Hitler asked Maria for a kiss. Maria declined, whereupon Hitler stepped back, shot out his arm in the Nazi salute and snapped, "Heil Hitler."

Strangely, this pair had a few more dates, but the affair came to nothing. Hitler broke it off on the advice of associates who pointed out that it was unseemly for a thirty-seven-year-old man to go around with a teenage girl.

This was not an isolated incident. Hitler also managed to get himself involved with Henny Hoffmann, the teenage daughter of Heinrich Hoffmann, the Nazi photographer. According to subsequent gossip, Hitler persuaded Henny to gratify his masochistic perversion; she then reported the episode to her father.

Enraged, Hoffmann went to Hitler, but came away with the exclusive right to take and license photographs of the Fuehrer, a privilege that subsequently earned him a fortune. This arrangement (see chapter 24, "Private Finances") was evidently quite satisfactory on both sides, because Hoffmann was never assassinated, a fate that frequently befell people who might be in a position to make trouble for Hitler.

As for Henny, she was subsequently married to Baldur von Schirach, head of the Nazi Youth and generally reputed to be a homosexual.

Hitler was also supposed to have had an involvement of some sort with Jenny Haug, the sister of one of his chauffeurs, but the overwhelmingly important relation-

ship of this period is that which he had with a young
woman named Angela Raubal. He called her "Geli," and
she called him "Uncle Alfi." With good reason. She was
the daughter of his half sister.

The exact nature of their physical relationship—if
any—will never be known but it was obvious that Hitler
dominated her life with a suffocating possessiveness.
She could go nowhere, see no one without Uncle Alfi's
permission.

On the afternoon of September 17, 1931, Geli shot
and killed herself.

Hitler was devastated by her death, brooded for
weeks, and talked of killing himself. Unfortunately, he
eventually recovered from his depression and found the
strength to go on. His revolting self-centeredness manifested itself in remarks he made to a friend at this time:
"Now I am altogether free, inwardly and outwardly.
Perhaps it was meant to be this way. Now I belong only
to the German people and my mission. But poor Geli!
She had to sacrifice herself for this."

He continued going to the theater, though, including
music halls and light opera. He particularly relished
performances featuring nearly—and sometimes completely—nude young women, and made frequent use of
opera glasses for a close-up look.

After he became Chancellor, he continued to visit the-
aters, but also had dancers perform at private Chancellery parties.

Stage and screen actresses were regularly invited to
both the private parties and official receptions. One of
these women, Renate Mueller, later told a friend that
after one of these affairs, the Fuehrer had gotten her

alone in a room, and it had seemed clear to her they were on their way to bed. Both undressed. Then Hitler threw himself to the floor and begged her to kick him. She refused but he, insisting on his utter unworthiness, begged for his "punishment." Mueller finally gave in and kicked him repeatedly, which, she says, greatly excited him.

During this period, Hitler reportedly had liaisons, presumably of a similar nature, with a number of other women. Throughout, however, he maintained a relationship with the woman who ultimately became his wife—Eva Braun.

Eva

Hitler frequently expressed the opinion that important men like himself did not need or want intelligent women for company, a remark he made even in the presence of women guests. Eva Braun filled the bill perfectly. She was young, athletic, and had no intellectual interests whatsoever.

Hitler had met her in 1929 when she was working as an assistant to Heinrich Hoffmann, the photographer father of Henny.

Eva's involvement with Hitler was an on and off matter, entirely at his whim, a situation which drove her to two suicide attempts. Perhaps these had some effect on Hitler because in 1936 he allowed her to move in with him. She was given her own room in his mountain villa, with a door leading to his bedroom.

As to what went on in that bedroom—Eva reportedly told a friend, "I have nothing from him as a man." Hitler himself once said, "It is true I have overcome the urge to physically possess a woman." He may have been impotent, or able to gratify himself only through his masochistic perversion. On the other hand, after examining the evidence—primarily the memoirs of aides and associates—some historians conclude Eva and Hitler had a conventional sex life. All in all, although an immense amount has been written about Hitler's sex life, it must be pointed out that all is reconstruction and speculation.

It is certain that Eva Braun eventually became Frau Hitler. The marriage took place shortly after midnight on April 29, 1945, barely an hour after Hitler had Eva's brother-in-law shot on a charge of treason.

Approximately thirty-six hours after the wedding, to avoid capture by the Russians, Hitler and Eva killed themselves.

Klara

It may seem grotesque to include Hitler's mother, Klara, among his "women." She did, however, have an unusual presence in his life, a fact of which Hitler's other women must have always been aware. She died in 1907, but Hitler carried her picture with him throughout his life and always hung her portrait in his bedroom, over his bed.

TWELVE
William Patrick Hitler

People are not to know who I am. They are not to know where I come from or about my family background.

—HITLER

Hitler wanted the world to regard him as unique in every respect, a remote "historic" figure without ties to a mundane life, such as relatives. He had them, though, and some of their stories shed a revealing light.

Paula Hitler

Hitler's sister, Paula, was his one full-blooded sibling. She told him he was crazy when he set out on his political career, and predicted he would wind up with his neck in a noose. This led to cool relations but not complete estrangement.

Paula eked out a meager living as a stenographer, working for an insurance company. As Hitler became successful, he began to send her a small monthly allowance, asking only one thing in return. As part of his effort to keep his relatives as anonymous as possible, he requested that she adopt the name he used when he wished to be incognito. Paula Hitler became Paula Wolf.

Hitler's household was managed by Angela Raubal, his half-sister (see below) until they quarreled, sometime in the autumn of 1936. There are different accounts as to the cause of the quarrel, but the upshot was that Angela left and her place was taken by Paula.

Although generally regarded as dull to the point of stupidity, Paula is probably unique among the members of Hitler's inner circle in that she managed to do some good. After the war, it was learned that on a number of occasions she had interceded with her brother and saved the lives of people scheduled for execution on anti-Nazi charges.

Angela Raubal

Hitler's father had been married twice before he married Klara Poelzl, who became the mother of Adolf and Paula. Angela was a daughter by the second marriage and was therefore Adolf's half sister. (She eventually married a man named Raubal.)

Despite the quarrel between them, Hitler came to her aid during the war, when her son Leo was taken prisoner on the Russian front. As it happened, the Germans had captured one of Stalin's sons. Through intermediaries, Hitler proposed an exchange but Stalin turned him down, saying, "I cannot do it. War is war."

Leo survived Russian captivity and eventually returned home. Stalin's son was not so fortunate; the Germans shot him.

Alois Hitler, Jr.

Angela's brother, and Adolf's half brother, was Alois
Hitler, Jr. He became a waiter but was also a thief who
was sent to jail at least twice.

In 1909, Alois emigrated to Ireland and then England,
where he married and fathered a child, William Patrick
Hitler (see below). In 1913 he abandoned his English
family, returned to Germany and started another family.
(He was later convicted of bigamy but was spared jail
when his first wife dropped the charge.)

When, in 1933, Adolf became Chancellor, Alois
opened a Berlin cafe with souvenir menu cards featuring
the name of the proprietor: "A. Hitler." Adolf tried to
put a stop to this by declaring the place off-limits to
Nazi Party members. The issue was finally resolved by
Alois closing the cafe and opening a new one, called the
"Tea Room Alois."

In May 1945, Alois fell into the hands of the British
occupying forces but was released after it was determined he had had no involvement in Nazi politics or
atrocities. The official British statement concludes with
the observation that Alois was "absolutely scared stiff
of being associated in any way with the Fuehrer's activ-
ities."

William Patrick Hitler

William Patrick was Adolf's English nephew, the son
left behind by Alois when he returned to Germany in
1913. He grew up to become an inconspicuous London
bookkeeper.

By 1931, Adolf had become an international figure about whom the world was developing an insatiable curiosity; William was given a contract by the Hearst newspaper chain for a story about Hitler's family and childhood.

In fact, William knew little about Adolf, so he wrote to his father in Germany, asking for information and anecdotes. The reply came not from Alois but from Adolf—tickets and a summons to Munich for him and his mother.

In a stormy meeting, Adolf told William it was essential that nothing about the family background be disclosed. He did not seem to fear anything in particular; he just did not want the family written about. To settle the matter, he offered William and his mother money (which William later claimed was diverted by Alois). That left the problem of what to tell the Hearst reporters.

Hitler's solution was to concoct a particularly improbable lie. He got William to agree to say there had been a mix-up and that his uncle, although named Adolf Hitler, was not *the* Adolf Hitler. There is no record of William having told the Hearst people this, or their reaction.

William and his mother returned to England, but after Hitler became Chancellor in 1933, William came back to Germany. This time, Hitler tried to convince him that Alois had only been adopted into the Hitler family, and therefore William really was not his nephew.

William checked up on this story and was able to quickly disprove it. Hitler thereupon ordered a job found for him.

He was placed in a minor position at the Opel Automobile Company but continued to appeal to Hitler for help from time to time. Finally, in 1938, Hitler decided he had had enough. Word was passed to William to leave Germany while he still could.

William returned to England and then went on to the United States, where he took to the lecture circuit, speaking about Hitler and Nazi Germany. In 1944, he enlisted in the U.S. Navy, from which he was honorably discharged in 1946.

There is a final, peculiar twist to his story. According to the historian John Toland, William did not change his notorious surname until after his return to civilian life, when he married. The couple produced a child, a boy, and named him Adolf.

Hitler's Children

In 1977, the historian Werner Maser announced he had found Hitler's son, a fifty-nine-year-old man fathered by Hitler when he was a soldier fighting in France in the First World War. This claim is not generally accepted, and none of the other occasionally circulated stories about a Hitler son or daughter have ever been substantiated.

Throughout his career, Hitler repeatedly asserted that he would have liked to have had children of his own, and he was energetically affectionate to those he knew, hoisting the small sons and daughters of associates onto his lap and watching indulgently as they romped on the great terrace of his mountain villa.

He may have been looking at the children but as usual, Hitler was thinking of himself. His remarks on the subject reek with his characteristic self-serving sentimentality. For example:

> How very much I too would like to have a family, children, children! Oh, God, you know how much I love children . . . But I have to deny myself this happiness. I have another bride—Germany!

It is hardly necessary to point out that his love for children did not extend to Jewish children or, for that matter, to anyone of any age whom he hated or who simply had the misfortune to be in his way. On the other hand, some suffered precisely because Hitler thought they might be useful.

As the Germans overran Europe, they engaged in systematic kidnapping. Children judged to be racially "pure"—with blue eyes and blond hair—were taken from their families and brought to special camps, to be raised as super-Nazis.

Likewise, women who happened to meet the crackpot Nazi criteria were also kidnapped (although some actually volunteered) for the breeding program. But these baby factories were also extermination camps. If a newborn child fell short of Nazi-defined perfection, it was likely to be killed.

Surviving infancy did not assure that the child would be spared pain and death at the hands of Nazi doctors. It is not uncommon for the blue eyes and blond hair of a child to darken within its first year. To diagnose what was "going wrong" in such cases, gruesome surgeries and other medical experiments were performed by sadistic perverts like Dr. Josef Mengele.

These abominable atrocities were entirely consistent with Hitler's philosophy, even when the victims were German children. He did not mean it affectionately when he said, "For my part, I must say that when I meet children, I think of them as though they were my own. They all belong to me."

On another occasion he said that a sacrifice of eighty to ninety percent of all German children was acceptable if the result were the purifying of German blood and the strengthening of the German race.

One of Hitler's last public appearances involved children. As the Russians were fighting their way through the rubble of Berlin, he ventured into the yard just outside his bunker to award medals of valor to the child soldiers—some only twelve years old—enlisted in the last ditch defense of the city.

He knew that in encouraging these children, he was sentencing them to almost certain death. But their efforts would postpone the end by some small degree, and there was always the chance of an intervening miracle. And when the end finally did come, to Hitler the children were just Germans who had failed him, and for whom he had no further use.

THIRTEEN

Hitler the Hypochondriac

Open the windows quickly, it smells here!

—PRINCESS CECILE,
ABOUT HITLER'S FLATULENCE

Terror, warmongering, mass murder on a scale almost beyond comprehension—but when it came to himself, Hitler was a whining hypochondriac.

For years, the problems he complained loudly and constantly about were relatively minor digestive disorders, mainly stomach cramps and chronic flatulence. The "man of destiny" could, and often did, fill a room with his odor.

Despite a staff of doctors, he treated himself with patent medicines which probably did more harm than good. He was persuaded to give up one of these when it was discovered to contain poisonous wood alcohol, but remained faithful to another nostrum, "Dr. Koester's Antigas pills." This contained small amounts of atropine and strychnine.

The manufacturer recommended taking three pills, three times a day. Having somehow been separated from them for two days, Hitler tried to catch up by downing

71

eighteen at once, to the horror of his doctors. Unfortunately, nothing much happened.

Hitler was possessed of a robust constitution and, at least until the early 1940s, his general health was excellent. He was, however, seized by fits of hypochondria and kept doctors on standby at all times.

He particularly feared cancer, the disease that had killed his mother, and was terrified when, in May 1935, a polyp was discovered and removed from his larynx. It proved benign.

A new complaint appeared—a leg rash so severe he had to give up wearing boots. Because his regular doctors were unable to cure this, he turned to Theodor Morell, a successful society doctor who nevertheless struck at least one Hitler associate as "a bit of a screwball."

Morell concluded that Hitler's skin and stomach problems were both caused by the same thing—a deficiency of the bacteria normally found in the intestine. The cure would take a year, he told Hitler, but he promised success.

Hitler regularly swallowed the capsules Morell prescribed, knowing full well they contained bacteria cultivated from human feces. Sometimes the capsules dissolved in Hitler's stomach instead of his intestine, and this caused him severe nausea.

Fortunately for Morell, Hitler's leg rash disappeared and his stomach cramps abated. Although they were to return later, the success was sufficient to assure Morell preeminence among Hitler's doctors.

Decline

Hitler remained vigorous through the early phase of the war, but as his armies began to meet defeat in Russia and elsewhere, his health deteriorated. Always something of an insomniac, he now did not even try going to bed before four or five in the morning, then tossed and turned until getting up again around eleven.

Formerly given to long trips in open cars and spur-of-the-moment picnics, he began to insist on staying indoors as much as possible, to protect himself from what he called "fresh air poisoning."

The stomach cramps intensified. Hitler had enough insight to recognize his affliction might be psychosomatic, a view he expressed with characteristic savagery, saying he was sure his gut would feel better if only he could execute the generals who had betrayed him. (The betrayal he referred to on this occasion was the fact that they had been defeated by the Russians.)

Drugs and Other Treatments

According to Ernst Schenck, another doctor on Hitler's staff, "Hitler was not a drug addict in the strict sense of the term . . . But he was psychologically dependent upon the *idea* of drugs as magic."

Schenck's records indicate that through the war years, Hitler was medicated with a staggering total of ninety-two different kinds of injections, pills and lotions. He took drugs to sleep and to stay awake. After 1943, Morell gave him an almost daily energy boosting shot, a mixture of vitamins, glucose and caffeine. Morell also supplied a pill made especially for Hitler and wrapped in gold foil, just like the chocolates of which he was so fond. (See chapter 14, "Hitler's Diet.") These pills, which Hitler took up to eight times a day, contained vitamins and amphetamines.

Hitler had high blood pressure, and for this, Morell resorted to an ancient method that was supposed to reduce the pressure by reducing blood volume—blood-sucking leeches.

To relieve constipation, enemas were prescribed. Hitler refused any assistance with these, insisting on administering them himself.

The Tremor

Early in 1943, an old affliction reappeared—a tremor in his left leg and arm. This had occurred once before, after the failure of his 1923 uprising.

The tremor that now began stopped a few times, but always resumed. One of the remissions occurred on July 20, 1944, the day he was very nearly assassinated by a bomb planted by rebellious generals. The blast killed others in the room, wounded him, and stopped the tremor. This confounding phenomenon may be explained by Hitler's psychology. He interpreted his being spared from death as confirmation that Providence intended him to survive and triumph, and this gave him an enormous boost.

As the war continued to worsen for Germany, the tremor returned.

Largely because of the tremor, Hitler is sometimes described as having Parkinson's disease. If correct, this might be a historically significant diagnosis, because Parkinson's is a neurological affliction which can affect decision-making.

The diagnosis is disputed by many historians and medical experts, whose analyses include the fact that Parkinson tremors do not abate, as Hitler's did.

Himmler, head of the S.S., suspected Hitler was experiencing the effects of advanced syphilis. He was evidently unaware of a Wassermann blood test administered in January 1940, which found no evidence of the disease in Hitler.

There is no debate that Hitler seemed to deteriorate at about the same rate as his empire. His hair turned gray, the tremor spread from his arm to his leg and eventually over to his right side. He stooped and then shuffled as he walked. Electrocardiograms revealed he was suffering a rapid hardening of the arteries and gave some evidence he may have had one or more small, unnoticed heart attacks. In February 1945, a minor stroke occurred which may have hastened his overall deterioration. In his final days, saliva drooled more or less continuously from the sides of his mouth.

Did Hitler's diseases—or his massive medications—affect his character and his competence?

His competence had always been in politics rather than in generalship. It is true that the defeat of France had assured him a great military reputation among his sycophants, but France probably failed as much from internal weakness as from any brilliant German stroke. Almost all of Hitler's other military schemes led to cataclysm.

It seems clear his medical decline followed his military failures, rather than causing them.

And it is certain that his character was unaffected by his medical history, for he remained ruthless, vindictive and murderous to the very end.

FOURTEEN

Hitler's Diet

In Hitler's biography, even commonplace details have pathological significance. His diet is no exception.

He began experimenting with vegetarianism in early adulthood, but for years was far from absolute in his adherence. In the early, frantic days of Nazi organizing, he was often too busy to sit down to a full meal. He ate on the run, gnawing chunks of sausage and slices of bread he carried in his pockets.

Suddenly, in September 1931, he manifested an active loathing for meat, saying, "It is like eating a corpse!" Revolted by the sight of stew, he had to leave the table.

The onset of this loathing followed the suicide of Geli Raubal, the niece with whom he had been in love. After she shot herself, Hitler took the extraordinary step of attending her autopsy. That marked the end of meat eating for him, with very few exceptions.

In time, his revulsion subsided sufficiently that he was

able to eat his vegetarian meals while others at the table had their goulash or sauerbraten. He thought it amusing, though, to try to spoil their pleasure with morbid jokes. He called beef broth corpse tea, and offered to have a pudding made from his blood.

His breakfast, lunches and dinners all tended to be made up of more or less the same foods. A typical day's consumption included eggs prepared in any of a number of ways, spaghetti, baked potatoes with cottage cheese, oatmeal, stewed fruits, and vegetable puddings. Meat was not completely excluded. Hitler continued to eat a favorite dish, *leberkloesse* (liver dumplings).

Vegetarian meals can be dull but Hitler's cook, Marlene Kunde, created non-meat dishes he found delectable. She had formerly been employed by the Rumanian dictator Atonescu, who had sung her praises and earned Hitler's gratitude by suggesting he hire her.

All went well until Heinrich Himmler, head of the S.S., informed the Fuehrer that he would have to dispense with Fraulein Kunde. Himmler had discovered she was a Jew.

Hitler told Himmler he had to be wrong. She was too good a cook, and she was respectful. In any event, he could not do without her.

Himmler persisted, producing irrefutable evidence.

Hitler countered by ordering the Kunde family "aryanized," declared non-Jewish . . . but a story this striking could not be contained. Rather than have it generally known he had a Jewish cook, Hitler finally fired her. No record exists of her ultimate fate.

Sweet Tooth

Hitler was always worried about gaining weight. "Imagine me going around with a potbelly," he said. "It would mean political ruin." Nevertheless, he consumed pastry and candy, particularly chocolates, in enormous quantities. He ate two pounds of chocolate a day, sometimes interrupting a conference to leave the room and eat a few chocolates before resuming. He also drank hot chocolate, topped with what one observer described as "a floating iceberg of whipped cream."

Hitler is also recorded as regularly putting seven teaspoons of sugar in his tea, and his friend Hanfstaengl once noticed him adding sugar to a glass of wine.

Teetotaler?

For purposes of propaganda among the German people, Hitler was depicted as living a sparse, ascetic life. This was entirely untrue. As part of the myth, it was said he abstained entirely from alcohol. This also was untrue, although his drinking was moderate. He sipped wine and beer occasionally; the beer was often a custom brew made for him with an alcohol content of less than 2 percent. Sometimes he added cognac to his tea.

He gave different reasons for his moderation. In one conversation, he cast himself in a martyr's role, claiming he refrained out of respect for the poor, who could not afford liquor.

On another occasion he explained his abstinence with a peculiar story from his adolescence. To celebrate the end of final exams, he had gone carousing with school-mates, gotten drunk for the first and only time in his life, and passed out in a field.

The next morning, he realized he had lost the certificate given him on completing the exams. When he went back to the school to get a duplicate, he learned he was in deep disgrace. The original certificate had been found in a field, torn into four squares and soiled. He had used it as toilet paper.

The school's director gave Hitler a dressing-down which remained a humiliation to him throughout his life. Nearly forty years later he said of that day, "I made a promise to myself that I would never get drunk again and I've kept my promise."

According to his valet, Hitler's favorite drink was tea, particularly peppermint and camomile. He refrained from coffee, saying he loved the smell of it but that it kept him from sleeping.

Eating with Hitler

Hitler's mealtime guests were served meat courses while he had his vegetarian dishes, but there were other constraints that made eating with him something less than a relaxing experience. Conversations between guests were conducted in a half whisper because everyone was on guard, ready to fall silent the moment the Fuehrer might open his mouth to speak. That would mark the end of conversation and the beginning of a Hitler monologue about almost anything other than the current political or military situation. Hitler forbade discussion of these topics over meals.

Another cause for mealtime tension was Hitler's fear of being poisoned. He felt safe enough at home, even with a Jewish cook, but at his field headquarters and elsewhere he had food tasters sample every dish.

This fear of poisoning was not a new obsession. In 1923, when Hanfstaengl visited him on his birthday, he found Hitler's room filled with delicacies sent by admirers, including cakes decorated with whipped cream eagles and swastikas. Hitler had sampled nothing, explaining to Hanfstaengl that these tempting delicacies might be poisoned . . . though not by the people who had sent them. The building he lived in was owned by Jews, and Jews, said Hitler, had ways of dripping poison down the walls and into the food.

No Smoking!

Smoking was forbidden in the Fuehrer's presence. Somehow he had become unalterably opposed to tobacco in any form but it is unclear how he reached this conclusion because he had bizarre ideas about human anatomy. When he tried to persuade his housekeeper, Anni Winter, to give up smoking, she suggested nicotine couldn't be worse than all the medical injections he was getting (see chapter 13, "Hitler the Hypochondriac"). He replied by patiently explaining these shots did no damage because "the fluid goes directly into my veins."

At his order, cigarettes were removed from the Christmas packages distributed to German soldiers and replaced with candy, and he considered requiring that in the future all cigarettes be manufactured without nicotine.

No More Rules

In the last few days of April 1945, as the Russians closed
in on Berlin, the people around Hitler began to smoke
quite openly. Eva Braun (see chapter 11, "Hitler's
Women") puffed on a small cigar. It was as significant
a sign as any that they all knew the game was up and
Hitler would soon be dead. Someone served him a meat
meal, and he ate it.

FIFTEEN

I Was Hitler's Dentist

I was the big man.

—DR. HUGO BLASCHKE

After the war, Allied and Russian investigators interviewed everyone they could find who had had anything whatsoever to do with Hitler. Even his barber, Arthur Wollenhaupt, was interrogated and he obliged his questioners by reporting that the savage dictator was frightened by haircuts. According to Wollenhaupt, Hitler sat "still as a lamb," nervously tensed as his hairline was trimmed. He also testified that Hitler always shaved himself because he could not bear the thought of anyone near his throat with a razor. Although stories like these may seem too satisfying to be true, Hitler's valet, Heinz Linge, happened to confirm the latter detail by mentioning Hitler's fear of the razor in an entirely separate interrogation.

Blaschke

Hitler's dentist, Hugo Blaschke, reported that Hitler maintained his composure during treatment. The problem was getting him in the chair.

Hitler cleaned his teeth meticulously but, perhaps because of the enormous amounts of sugar he consumed, they were yellow and rotten. Many had been replaced with porcelain or gold, and when he smiled he habitually brought his hand up to block a view of his mouth. Although not apparent in most published photographs, one gold tooth gleamed dully from the front of his upper jaw.

Because of the chronically poor condition of Hitler's teeth, Blaschke recommended check-ups every three or four months. Not only did Hitler refuse to allow this, he put off visits even when he had a toothache. His first resort was always drugs. Only if these failed to kill the pain would Blaschke be called.

American Trained

Ironically, Hitler's dentist was American-trained. Blaschke had been born and raised in Germany but went to the University of Pennsylvania to study dentistry.

The school yearbook reveals his nickname there was the "Count"; as his personal motto he selected "Knowledge is Power." He graduated in 1911 and returned to Germany.

One may wonder how the minor figures, such as Hitler's dentist, felt about their service to so evil a character.

As it happens, Blaschke was a Nazi. He joined the Party in 1931, well before Hitler came to power.

He became Hitler's dentist in 1934, recommended by Hermann Goering and other top Nazis who were already patients. Summoned when the Fuehrer was attacked by one of the toothaches drugs could not quell, he was able to relieve the pain quickly and thus became, in his own words, "the big man."

After the war, one of Blaschke's interrogators could not resist pointing out that had he remained in America he would undoubtedly now be enjoying a prosperous retirement instead of being destitute and interned. Blaschke admitted this was so. Then he paused, his eyes taking on what his questioner later described as a misty shine. "But on the other hand," said Blaschke, "then I would never have been Hitler's dentist."

This particular interview took place in 1947, by which time no one could have any excuse for ignorance about the enormity of Hitler's crimes. Nevertheless, it seems that for some people nothing could dim Hitler's glamour.

The Dental Records

Minor figures can unlock major mysteries.

Immediately after the war, Blaschke had been questioned with the hope he could supply dental details which would be invaluable in identifying Hitler's remains, should they ever be discovered.

Blaschke had fallen into Western hands, but his office, records and assistants had been taken by the Russians, and they refused to supply copies of anything to the West. At the time this only seemed consistent with standard Russian policy but it is now believed to have been part of a Russian plot to make a mystery of Hitler's demise. Working from memory, Blaschke was able to give a detailed description of Hitler's teeth and dentures, and even molded plaster models of them.

The models were subsequently lost, but the interrogation report survived and a quarter of a century later became a vital piece of evidence in resolving the question of when and where Hitler died (see chapter 32, "Hitler's Corpse").

SIXTEEN

Hitler's Wardrobe

It was with great reluctance that I had definitely to give up wearing leather shorts.

—HITLER

Even in the choice of his clothes, Hitler manifested his violence, calculation, and selfishness.

He felt comfortable in *lederhosen*, the leather shorts which are part of the traditional south German country costume. He thought so highly of them as emblematic of the national identity that he suggested to Himmler that special units of the S.S. might wear them, a recommendation this devoted sycophant managed to overlook.

Hitler abandoned *lederhosen* because in the cities of northern Germany they would have made him look like a country bumpkin. But he would not have been himself if he had not complained repeatedly about having had to do this. Quoted out of context, it might appear as though he were joking, but he was serious when he said that giving up *lederhosen* "was one of the biggest sacrifices I had to make."

With the possible exception of his leather shorts, all of Hitler's pants had one thing in common—an extra pocket specially sewn in. This was for the pistol he carried at all times.

On occasion, before becoming Chancellor, he did wear a conventional cartridge belt and holster. Visiting a friend's house for dinner, he politely hung the holster and belt on the hallway coatrack before sitting down to eat.

Bulletproof?

To many contemporaries, Hitler's upper body seemed bulky, but not with the fullness of healthy athletic development. Some said his clothes were padded to make him look physically impressive; others believed the bulk was a bulletproof vest. The latter explanation is entirely possible, even likely, in the light of another, more certainly established detail—Hitler's armored hat.

According to witnesses who handled it, at least one of his military hats was "heavy as a cannonball" because it was lined with about three and a half pounds of steel.

Tailoring

During the years of struggle to achieve power, Hitler deliberately cultivated an ill-tailored look to emphasize the "common man" element of his appeal. There may have been another purpose as well. Kurt Ludecke was not alone among Hitler's associates when he wondered "if Hitler's utterly mediocre appearance was not one of his greatest assets, leading his enemies to habitually underestimate him."

Throughout his career, Hitler wore trench coats rather

than bourgeois overcoats, a reminder to all of his days as a soldier during World War One. For Party rallies and parades, he donned the familiar brownshirt uniform of the Storm Troopers. Other occasions called for nothing more spectacular than an ordinary business suit. After he became Chancellor, diplomatic events sometimes required striped pants, tails and top hat, an outfit he neither felt nor looked comfortable in.

When he attended the Olympic winter games he and his entourage all appeared in long black leather overcoats. Hitler's, though, was subtly different. It had been specially burnished to a higher sheen than the others. He was made to seem a source of warmth and light.

Haberdashery

Perhaps because he couldn't be bothered—it seems incredible he was this inept—Hitler often used pre-tied ties.

He wore a calf-length nightshirt to bed and didn't own a pair of pajamas until his forty-ninth birthday, when Eva Braun gave him a dozen pair. All were blue and white, the colors of Bavaria, where he had had his first great political successes.

One hot, muggy afternoon in July 1944, Hitler nearly lost his life in the bomb blast set by rebellious generals. His trousers were shredded and it was thus incidentally revealed that even in humid summer weather the Fuehrer wore full-length white underwear.

A few days later, he sent the singed and torn remains of his uniform to Eva Braun. It had great significance,

he said, because it demonstrated the force of the blast
and proved that Providence protected him.

The Sacred Coat

Throughout the war, Hitler wore Army uniforms of one
kind or another, rather than Nazi Party uniforms or civilian clothes. This was literal fulfillment of a promise
he had made the German people when he announced the
invasion of Poland and the beginning of the Second
World War. He said that now he would put on the soldier's coat, "the most sacred and dear to me," and would
not take it off "until victory is secured, or I will not
survive the outcome." He was wearing his Army tunic
when he killed himself on April 30, 1945, making this
one of the few promises he ever kept.

SEVENTEEN

Hitler's Bookshelf

Hitler was simply on thorns to see each new issue of the Stuermer. *It was the one periodical that he always read with pleasure, from the first page to the last.*

—HERMANN RAUSCHNING,
EARLY HITLER ASSOCIATE

itler's appetite for newspapers was insatiable, compulsive. Colleagues complained he would break off a conversation in midsentence if he caught sight of a fresh newspaper lying on a table.

Without doubt, his favorite paper was the *Stuermer* (Storm Trooper), a grossly obscene and sadistic anti-Semitic Nazi weekly. Hitler looked forward eagerly to each new issue.

Sources

As a young man living in Vienna before the First World War, Hitler was a devoted reader of a series of anti-Semitic pamphlets titled *Newsletters of the Blond Champions of Man's Rights*. These propounded a bizarre world view in which "Germanic man" battled against Jews to restore racial purity in the world. Among the tactics employed by Jews in this scenario was poisoning German bloodlines by raping blond women.

Hitler was also devoted to the writings of one Guido von List, who had similar ideas but added that the triumph of racial purity could be achieved through political means.

Some time during his Vienna years, the young Hitler carefully studied a pioneering book on an altogether different subject—mass psychology. This was *The Crowd*, by Gustave Le Bon, a nineteenth-century psychologist who was one of the first to point out that individuals in a large group lose the ability to think and are most effectively persuaded with crude simplifications endlessly repeated.

Le Bon suggested that a leader who wanted to control his followers ought to create a movement with pseudo-religious overtones and spectacular mass rallies.

Because Hitler propounded these ideas in *Mein Kampf* without crediting Le Bon (see chapter 3, "Hitler's Book"), some amateur analysts mistakenly conclude Hitler was an innovative genius of propaganda.

Although Hitler clearly was capable of learning from books, generally he did not read to learn but to confirm opinions he already held. He customarily began a book by looking at its end and would read the whole of it only if he agreed with the author's conclusions.

Truth was irrelevant. He was wildly enthusiastic about a book called *The Protocols of the Elders of Zion*, which purported to be a secret Jewish agenda for the takeover of the world. When one of his associates pointed out that the *Protocols* had long been exposed as a fraud, created by the Russian secret police under the Tsar, Hitler replied by saying that did not matter because of the work's "intrinsic truth."

Daily Reading

Hitler's personal library included encyclopedias, histories, biographies and books on war. One of his secretaries later recalled that nothing in his collection reflected an interest in literature. His friend Hanfstaengl noticed illustrated works of a "semi-pornographic" nature which, he reports, were well-thumbed.

For his routine daily reading, in addition to newspapers, Hitler relied on magazines, including those in foreign languages if they contained military facts and photographs. During the war his most important daily reading became a loose-leaf catalogue of German weapons and ammunition types, kept scrupulously current by aides who inserted regularly revised pages.

Hitler used this book as a weapon against his own general staff. During military conferences he made sure the agenda gave him the opportunity to demonstrate his knowledge, as though he carried every aspect of the war, down to the smallest details, in his head. In fact, he was citing selections he had specially memorized the night before. This simple trick added to the aura of omniscience which, with few exceptions, thoroughly intimidated his generals and admirals.

This was all to the good. Despite his grasp of facts and figures, Hitler was more often wrong than right about military matters. Had he listened to his advisors instead of winning arguments with them, the German armed forces might have done even more damage than they did.

Cowboys and Indians

Racist tracts, pornography, studies of war and propaganda, immense amounts of raw data about armaments ... but there was one set of books Hitler may have admired above all. These were the cowboy and Indian novels of Karl May, a German who had never been to America. Hitler adored them as a child, and was still re-reading them in his adult years. Hermann Goering curried favor by presenting the Fuehrer with a complete set custom bound in vellum.

May's novels were much more than an incidental pleasure in Hitler's life. As it happens, they are not only fictional, but completely inaccurate. Hitler must not have known this because he gave them several astonishing endorsements. On one occasion, he said of May, "I owe him my first notions of geography, and the fact that he opened my eyes to the world."

He also urged his generals to study May's books for practical tips on combating guerrilla warfare, certain that this would ensure success on the Russian front. This foolishness is entirely consistent with an essential aspect of Hitler's character. For him, belief and fact were identical, and he would use anything to support an argument, even fantastic Westerns written by a man who had never been to America.

In summary—Hitler used books just as he used everything else in his life. He did not read for insight or simple pleasure. What he wanted was power and self-aggrandizement, and no contradictions.

EIGHTEEN

Hitler at the Movies

He had seen The Tunnel . . . *he was aflame with the idea that this was the way to found a new party.*

—REINHOLD HANISCH, EARLY
HITLER FRIEND

There is a certain fascination in the possibility that Hitler enjoyed pleasures most people can understand—like going to the movies. Hitler was an enthusiastic moviegoer, but not for reasons shared by the rest of the audience.

Inspiration

Throughout his career, Hitler's speeches were an essential and enormously effective part of his political appeal. It is ironic that the power of oratory may first have been suggested to him by a silent movie.

He saw it in Vienna in 1910. It was *The Tunnel*, about a great construction project and a labor revolt. The hero, who seizes control of the crowd and becomes its leader, does so by means of an inspired speech.

The twenty-one-year-old Hitler was greatly impressed. Shortly afterwards, he said to a friend that seeing *The Tunnel* made him realize that mastering public oratory could give a man the power to found a great political party.

Favorites

Hitler continued to be a consistent moviegoer. After he came to power, he had private screenings for himself and his inner circle at the Chancellery and his other residences, regularly watching two or three pictures a night.

His staff was not adept with the projector; the film sometimes snapped or came on upside down. Hitler remained good humored in the face of these mishaps, but if the movie bored or irritated him he often ordered the projectionist to move on to another film. On the other hand, if a film pleased him he was likely to have it run repeatedly.

British and American pictures were screened as well as German. Among Hitler's favorite stars were Emil Jannings, Greta Garbo and Shirley Temple.

He did not like Charlie Chaplin, even before Chaplin parodied him in *The Great Dictator*, and it is not known whether or not he ever saw this film.

One of his favorite movies was *Lives of a Bengal Lancer*, about British heroics in colonial India. Whereas most people see this simply as a rousing adventure film, Hitler admired it for its depiction of the successful domination of one race by another, and ordered that it be required viewing for the S.S.

He found *King Kong* spellbinding and talked about it

for days. On the night of March 15, 1939, after his sudden and utterly successful occupation of Czechoslovakia, he was seen proudly pacing the corridors of Prague's Hradcany Castle, beating his chest like a gorilla.

Specialty Items

Hitler, who seriously considered himself an expert on almost everything, routinely telephoned German motion picture studios with ideas for productions. Fortunately, he did not seem to mind when these were not acted on, and sometimes called for nothing more than small talk about studio life. Occasionally he visited the studios, to watch scenes being filmed and have lunch with the stars.

He did commission some films, but these were not for general release. They were pornographic items for his private viewing, of a kind, we are told, which would appeal only to a "perverted voyeur." The report does not include specific details.

One specially made film sheds light on Hitler's grotesquely twisted sentimentality. An admiring and, evidently, psychopathic Indian Maharaja sought to please the great German leader with a production featuring the slaughter of animals and people. This was not a fictional film. There were no special effects; everything was real.

Hitler's reaction was predictable only in part. He sat unmoved by scenes in which humans were torn apart by animals, but when the animals were killed in retaliation, he hid his eyes with his hand and asked to be told when the killing of the animals was over.

A Change of Habit

Some time after he managed to start the Second World War, Hitler announced that he would live up to a promise he had made the German people—that they would suffer no privation which he himself did not endure. He made no alterations in his diet or the comfort of his various residences, but he did forego his movies. The daily screening of feature films, however—British and American as well as German—was continued for his entourage.

He did watch the newsreels which chronicled the triumphant advance of Nazi forces on all fronts. The destruction of Warsaw by German dive bombers, for example, was filmed partly in slow motion and he found this footage enthralling.

In February 1943, Nazi forces suffered a shattering and pivotal defeat at Stalingrad. Thereafter, Hitler lost his taste for newsreels and ceased watching them. But he wasn't completely finished with films.

On July 20, 1944, he was nearly killed by a bomb planted in an assassination attempt by some top officers. Although wounded, he was not put out of action and he quickly had the would-be assassins rounded up. Many were taken to Berlin's Ploetzensee Prison, where they were slowly strangled to death by being hanged from meat hooks with piano wire. A newsreel crew filmed the death agonies, in color.

The film was then rushed to Hitler, who viewed it with relish and had it run over and over.

NINETEEN

Hitler Laughs

Hitler's laugh always had a flavor of derision and sarcasm.

—PAUL SCHMIDT,
HITLER'S INTERPRETER

Hitler was a crude but inventive mimic who often entertained his inner circle with a repertoire which included an impersonation of Eric Phipps, a key British diplomat. This routine, meant to ridicule his English formality, was so effective members of Hitler's staff found themselves barely able to keep a straight face during their meetings with Phipps. The effect of Hitler's mockery, thus, was to encourage a giddy contempt for one of the men trying to save Europe from war.

Hitler's allies were not exempt from his vulgarity. After one diplomatic reception, he convulsed his entourage with a caricature of Matsuoka, the Japanese Foreign Minister. The joke here was that Matsuoka was made out to be an ape.

Hitler was at his best when his subject was afflicted with a physical infirmity he could mock. Labor Chief

Robert Ley was a perfect foil, for he was both a stutterer and a drunk. Hitler had no end of fun with this.

A Hitler Joke

Occasionally, Hitler told jokes. Everyone knows about volts and amps but what, he asked, was the difference between a goebbels and a goering? (Joseph Goebbels was Minister of Propaganda; Hermann Goering was notorious for his love of fancy uniforms and medals.) The answer was that a goebbels was the amount of nonsense a man could talk in an hour; a goering, the amount of metal that could be pinned on his chest. Hitler told this joke frequently, often in the presence of these two men, whose discomfiture enhanced his enjoyment.

Hitler has been described as doubling over with laughter, laughing so hard tears came to his eyes, slapping his thighs or knees in delight, and giggling. More often than not, these fits of amusement were occasioned by accounts of humiliation and cruelty.

The Uses of Laughter

Goebbels was one of those around Hitler who learned to make skillful use of his ugly sense of humor. If a Goebbels rival happened to do something the least bit foolish, Goebbels scurried to Hitler with the tale. His pretext was that he was only providing an anecdote for the Fuehrer's amusement, but in fact he knew he was demolishing his competitor.

If the rival failed to present an opportunity for humiliation, Goebbels created one. He ruined one man's career by making him the butt of a series of practical jokes, including having him deliver a long radio speech into a dead microphone. When Goebbels told this story, Hitler laughed and laughed, and Goebbels knew his victim would never be considered for an important post.

Practical Jokes

Hitler hatched more than a few practical jokes of his own. A favorite target was his pompous Foreign Minister, Ribbentrop. More than once, he had an aide telephone Ribbentrop with an alarming report—the Fuehrer was furious about something he had done. Hitler stood close by during the call, listening with delight to Ribbentrop's agitation, whispering further instructions for driving the Foreign Minister to the edge of nervous collapse.

It is difficult to imagine any other national leader having such contempt for one of his own Ministers.

Backfire

One of Hitler's jokes backfired on him with significant effect. The butt in this case was Ernst Hanfstaengl, his old associate and Foreign Press Chief, who had made a remark which Hitler felt denigrated the German forces fighting in the Spanish Civil War. Some time later, in February 1937, after he had forgotten all about this conversation, Hanfstaengl was summoned for an important mission. He was to fly to Spain, to help Franco cultivate the foreign press.

On the way to the airfield, people in on the joke told him horrifying tales of atrocities supposedly committed by Franco's opponents. His anxiety was increased by something that happened just before he got on the plane, something that had never occurred before—he was helped into a parachute.

There were other passengers, but none of them had parachutes. And they were all obviously members of the Gestapo, the murderous Secret Police.

After the plane took off, the pilot invited Hanfstaengl up to the cockpit for a visit and quickly worked the conversation around to the purpose of the trip. When Hanfstaengl said he was to meet with Franco, the pilot feigned astonishment. His orders, he said, were to fly behind enemy lines in Spain, so Hanfstaengl could parachute in to do some kind of spy work.

Hanfstaengl was aghast—a terrible mistake had been made. Then it dawned on him. Hitler had decided to murder him, with the "heroic mission" as the cover-up.

The pilot was sympathetic when Hanfstaengl begged him to turn back, but argued there was nothing he could do. After all, he pointed out, the Gestapo was on board.

Hanfstaengl experienced about half an hour of sheer terror, and then a miracle occurred, a chance for escape. The pilot announced the plane had developed engine trouble. He was aborting the mission, they would land at the next available field.

When they landed, Hanfstaengl saw, to his immense relief, that they were still in Germany. Claiming he felt airsick and had to get to a toilet, he walked away from the group, and kept going. Before anyone could tell him the whole thing had been a joke, he was on a train that took him to Switzerland.

Hitler was beside himself because Hanfstaengl knew enough about him and the Nazi Party to make his defection dangerous. Messages were sent trying to persuade him to return but Hanfstaengl kept traveling, on to England and then the United States, where he did indeed become a valuable source of information.

Jokes About Hitler

It was a serious criminal offense in Nazi Germany to make an anti-Hitler joke, and it was not uncommon for people to be thrown into concentration camps or executed outright for doing so.

Nevertheless, people around Hitler sometimes made jokes to his face that would have been insulting to an honest man. One aide to Foreign Minister Ribbentrop told Hitler that Ribbentrop's staff had wanted to honor him with a jewel-encrusted chest filled with the treaties he had negotiated. They had to give up the plan, said the aide, when they realized Germany had broken all the treaties. Hitler roared with laughter.

Hitler Makes a Joke About Himself

In jokes, of course, there is frequently truth, especially when a man is joking about himself. Throughout his career, Hitler ground out endless diatribes justifying Germany's need to defend itself against a hostile world, but a single joke he made one evening concisely defined his real foreign policy. Aides were looking for a missing flashlight. Hitler good-naturedly disclaimed responsibility with a chilling crack that would be too blatant for historical fiction. "Look," he said, "I poach other people's countries—I don't pinch their flashlights!"

TWENTY

Games the Fuehrer Played

When we were children playing together, my brother Adolf was always the leader.

—PAULA HITLER

Childish games remained an integral part of Hitler's adult life. Some were harmless. There was, for example, the "dressing game," a self-challenge which began with his valet laying out his clothes for him in the morning, then waiting outside the room for his cry of "Starting!"

This was the signal for the valet to time him getting dressed; when he finished, Hitler checked eagerly to see if he had beaten his previous record.

Many of Hitler's games challenged not himself but his associates. A favorite, launched without warning, was to make direct eye contact and stare the other man down. On one occasion, over afternoon tea, a challenged associate, demonstrating rare courage, refused to look away . . . until Hitler turned and struck up a conversation with someone else at the table. He never acknowledged his defeat and didn't seem to hold it against the victor.

Hitler's games sometimes involved his entire entourage. As they traveled about the country, first in the course of acquiring power and then exercising it, they played "Beaver," the scoring word to be shouted by whoever first spotted a man with a beard. At the end of the trip the one who had made the most sightings won. That was usually Hitler.

The Appeasement Game

In some respects, Hitler's whole career was a game of challenge and bluff, particularly his foreign policy. Indeed, Daniel Ellsberg has used game theory to produce a revealing analysis of Hitler's pre-war diplomatic methods.

In game theory, rewards and risks are described for each possible move. For Hitler, the reward was usually territorial gain; the risk was the danger of setting off a war. For example, on March 7, 1936, he sent troops to occupy the Rhineland, a German border zone demilitarized at the end of the First World War.

Had the French opposed Hitler's move, he would have retreated. At that time, their forces were still greatly superior to his and he would have lost his gamble . . . for gambling was precisely what he was doing.

He had a peculiar advantage, a wild card. More precisely, *he* was the wild card. He was betting that the French would behave in a restrained and sane manner, but they had good reason, judging by his oratory and general behavior, to believe him crazy enough to fight, even against impossible odds. They backed down.

(Ellsberg's analysis of Hitler's strategy may itself have had far-reaching consequences, affecting U.S. policy on Vietnam. In *Without Fear or Favor*, Harrison Salisbury points out that Ellsberg presented his ideas in one of Henry Kissinger's Harvard seminars; some years later Nixon said to H. R. Haldeman, "I call it the Madman Theory . . . I want the North Vietnamese to believe I've reached the point where I might do *anything* to stop the war.")

Hitler's ultimate objective may have been insane, but his methods were not. Each time he made a demand he tantalized his opponents with a reward. Each time, he insisted this was his last demand. If the Allies acceded to it, they would have permanent peace. Seen from the other side of the board, The Hitler Foreign Policy Game can be called by its more common name, which is Appeasement.

The Allies may have been foolishly hopeful but by the time of the Czech crisis in the fall of 1938, they recognized they might have to fight to stop Hitler. By then, however, Hitler had managed to increase their risk. Now they faced not only the possibility of war, but of a war they might lose. Hitler had used the time to vastly enlarge the German war machine, and through his skillful playing of the Foreign Policy Game had, without losing men or material, gained strategic territorial advantages. The Rhineland, for example, would make an excellent jumping-off point for an attack on France.

Even if the Allies did win the war, Hitler had them convinced their losses would be catastrophic. At the very least, they could be sure their cities would be blasted into rubble by his mighty air force. Once again, the Allies backed down; Hitler got Czechoslovakia without a fight.

In fact, his air force was not quite what it seemed.

Musical Chairs

To insure the Allies would be demoralized by the potential of his overwhelming air power, Hitler had resorted to another kind of game—musical chairs. Foreign guests were given tours of German airfields, all of which were packed with enormous numbers of advanced fighters and bombers. What the visitors did not know was that the planes were being secretly flown from field to field, so that each plane would be counted many times.

Hitler's Real Game?

Hitler's strategy of seizing territory without war was proceeding with spectacular success, but as he planned the invasion of Poland the men around him grew anxious. Significantly, the language of games was used. Trying to dissuade him, Goering advised, "Let's stop trying to break the bank!" And Hitler replied, "It's the only game I've ever played—breaking banks."

In fact, it is likely Hitler had been playing another game all along. Both his enemies and most of his associates believed he was bluffing, using the threat of war to get what he wanted. Evidence which became available after the war, however, depicts him as restless and disappointed when his bluffs succeeded. It seems he relished the prospect of a gigantic contest, an ultimate game with everything at stake. He wanted to plunge Germany into war.

The Border Charade

Hitler's prewar conquests were preceded by elaborate justifications, usually claims of unbearable insults against the honor of the German people. Poland was no exception. To produce evidence of Polish provocation, he staged a hideous charade.

He announced that Polish soldiers had struck across the border and seized a German radio station before being driven back, leaving many of their dead behind. As evidence, foreign reporters were shown bullet-ridden corpses in Polish uniforms.

In fact, the dead men had been German concentration camp prisoners. Murdered by poisonous injections, their bodies had been dressed in Polish uniforms and taken to the border site, where bullets were fired into them.

Poland proved to be the trigger, the beginning of the game Hitler probably wanted to play all along. When he refused to pull back his invading force, France and Britain declared war. The bluffing was over.

TWENTY-ONE

Hitler and Music

For Adolf, nothing could compete with the great mystical world that the Master conjured up for us.

—AUGUST KUBIZEK, BOYHOOD FRIEND

Hitler didn't care much for Mozart, Beethoven or Bach. "The Master" whose music had the power to enthrall him was Richard Wagner. It may have been a Wagner opera that first excited his political ambition.

He was fifteen years old when he and his friend August Kubizek, both regular operagoers, first saw Wagner's *Rienzi*. Set in ancient Rome, the opera tells the story of a man who rises from the people and achieves heroic stature by leading them in a glorious, though ultimately futile revolution.

Usually, as Hitler and Kubizek left the theater after a performance, Hitler launched into an extensive critique of the musicians and the singers, but this time he was quiet. Kubizek tried to draw him out; Hitler told him to shut up.

Aside from the silence, they followed their usual routine, which included climbing a small hill on the outskirts of town. Everything was enshrouded in fog, but as they reached the top they found themselves suddenly clear of the mist. The stars overhead seemed to blaze . . . and at this dramatic moment, young Hitler broke his silence with talk Kubizek had never heard before. He spoke of a mandate that would some day be entrusted to him, to do as the heroic Rienzi had done. He would, he said, "lead his people out of servitude, to the heights of freedom." Kubizek had absolutely no idea what Hitler was talking about but later described this episode as "the most impressive hour I ever lived through with my friend."

The two remained close for a few years more but Hitler, though interested in politics, never said anything further about a political career, seeming to return completely to his dream of becoming an artist (see chapter 22, "The Art Dictator"). Decades later, when Hitler became Chancellor of Germany, Kubizek wrote a shy letter of congratulation, and Hitler summoned him for the first of what became a series of visits. During one of these, Kubizek reminded him of the *Rienzi* episode. This was just the stuff legends were made of. Hitler was delighted to be reminded of that night; the story became part of his regular repertoire. At its conclusion, with great portent and solemnity, he would say, "In that hour it began."

Rienzi may have inspired Hitler, but he also drew a practical lesson from it. The heroic Rienzi, although a man of the people, had enlisted allies from the aristocratic and wealthy classes. Hitler was making similar alliances on his way to power when a member of his inner circle cautioned that it was the conservative elements who had betrayed Rienzi and destroyed him. Hitler agreed but pointed out he was avoiding Rienzi's great mistake ... which was that Rienzi had not founded a Party of his own.

Music and the Party

Hitler ordered that the annual Nazi festival at Nuremberg always begin with a performance of Wagner's opera, *Die Meistersinger*. The 1933 Festival was to be a particularly significant one—the first since the Nazis had taken power. When Hitler entered the opera house, however, he was chagrined to find it nearly empty. His followers had not come to Nuremberg for culture.

Squads of Storm Troopers were dispatched to Nuremberg's cafes, beer halls and brothels with orders to round up an audience. Even these energetic efforts, though, proved insufficient to fill the house.

Hitler's devotion to Wagner was not exclusive. The fanfare from Verdi's *Aida* was used to begin the great stadium rallies, and the Fuehrer always made his grand entrance to the accompaniment of his personal motif, a swinging military number called the "Badenweiler March."

The Radio

"Badenweiler" was also used to alert radio listeners when Hitler was about to broadcast an address.

During the war, each military campaign was assigned a separate radio musical theme, to be used to precede victory announcements. A few bars of Liszt's *Les Pre-*

ludes, for example, was the fanfare Hitler chose for his
triumphs in Russia.

Lighter Music

Hitler enjoyed lighter music, including the operettas of
Strauss and Lehar. He was particularly fond of the latter's *The Merry Widow*, but this may have been because
of the way it was performed in Munich in the '30s. He
was entranced by an American dancer named Dorothy,
whipping out his opera glasses for a close-up look when
she did her famous "back-bending number." Sometimes
Dorothy wore transparent water wings and sometimes
nothing at all.

He also regularly visited a variety theater, The Metropole, but it wasn't just to get a look at the dancers. He
really did like the music.

At home, he had an enormous collection of phonograph records, and guests were likely to be subjected to
disc after disc of Wagner and other serious music. But
as soon as the guests were gone, Hitler would ask his
butler, Arthur Kannenberg, to entertain.

Kannenberg played the accordion and sang, and stuck
to popular tunes, including one of Hitler's great favor-
ites, "Who's Afraid of the Big Bad Wolf?"

Dance

Hitler approved of traditional nineteenth-century ballet,
but denigrated twentieth-century developments as mere
"acrobatics."

As for ballroom dancing, Hitler believed waltzes were

effeminate, and seriously argued that the Viennese passion for them was a factor in the downfall of the Austro-Hungarian Empire.

Whistling

Although Hitler refused to dance, he occasionally picked out tunes on the piano and experimented briefly with a harmonica and a flute.

His great musical capability was as a whistler. He could reproduce long passages from Wagner and others, usually with accuracy. On one occasion, though, he was challenged with the suggestion that he had gotten a passage wrong.

When the matter was put to a test with a record of the work in question, he had to admit his version was different from the composer's . . . but he insisted he was not wrong—it was the composer who had erred. Hitler didn't laugh when he said this and no one present was altogether sure he was joking.

TWENTY-TWO

The Art Dictator

Art is a Mission Demanding Fanaticism

—HITLER, INSCRIBED OVER THE
DOOR OF THE HOUSE OF
GERMAN ART, MUNICH

As a boy, Hitler dreamed of living a bohemian artist's
life, and as a young man he earned his living as a
painter. As Fuehrer, he had works of genius destroyed
by the thousands.

In 1907, the eighteen-year-old Hitler came to Vienna
from Linz, his hometown, to take the entrance exam for
the Painting School of the prestigious Academy of Fine
Art. The examination required him to demonstrate his
skill by illustrating classical themes such as "Cain and
Abel" and "Joy and Moonlight."

He did well enough to be allowed to submit his portfolio of original art for evaluation by the faculty.

To his shock, the portfolio was judged inadequate. He
was denied entrance.

The Academy's Director was sympathetic. Believing
Hitler had talent, he suggested applying to the School of
Architecture, but to be eligible for this Hitler would have

to complete high school work he had abandoned. This, he disdained and would not do.

A year later, armed with a new portfolio, he tried again as a painter but he never got to show his new work. This time, he failed the preliminary exam.

One legend of popular mythology has the young Hitler making a momentous, terrible turn from art to politics because of this rejection. We are tantalized with the prospect of a peaceful "Hitler the artist" who might have been.

In fact, the Academy's rejection did not seal his fate. His watercolors were good enough to be sold by dealers, and he earned additional income with commercial art. Sporadically, he turned out hand-painted postcards, advertising posters, and small paintings used by furniture-makers as inlaid decoration for chairs and sofas.

He could have made a satisfactory living from commercial art as he pursued fine art, despite the Academy's rejection. Many others did.

But Hitler did not care to work. Various dealers and, for a short while a partner, fell out with him, exasperated by his laziness and unreliability. He preferred to dream of glory. Increasingly, he spent his time arguing radical politics with fellow residents at his lodging house.

(In *Mein Kampf*, Hitler claims that during this time he learned about the problems of the ordinary working-man because he himself worked as a construction laborer. This is untrue and probably contributed to the popular misconception he was once a house painter or wallpaper hanger.)

Although Hitler mostly chose buildings and landscapes as subjects, one of his World War I sketches shows him and his comrades walking along a road in France. It must be said that the picture is lively, made almost whimsical by the soldier who carries an umbrella.

After the war Hitler, obsessed by the cataclysmic events he had survived, concentrated entirely on politics, but as he sat in meetings or over meals he continued to sketch. Generally, he turned out nothing more than doodles—occasionally, the heads of men and wolves; more often, circles, squares, fancy borders and, of course, swastikas.

Sometimes, as a kind of parlor trick, he drew famous buildings from memory. On occasion, he sketched structures he planned to build one day. As if it were needed, these latter are further evidence of the reach and durability of his ambitions. In 1925, when Germany was experiencing a measure of prosperity and Nazi prospects were consequently near their all-time low, Hitler produced the basic rendering for a monument he swore he would eventually build in Berlin—a German Arch of Triumph. It was to be ten times the size of the one in Paris. He never did get around to this, but he still had the sketch a decade later when he gave it to architect Albert Speer, to incorporate in designs for a new Berlin.

The Fuehrer as Critic

Hitler had very pronounced views as to what was acceptable in painting and what was not. He railed against anything not strictly representational, saying that artists who painted "green skies and blue meadows" either had eye trouble or were insane. He placed the blame for the spread of these hideous new styles on—the Jews. It was part of a plot, he said, to demoralize Gentiles by depicting everything in lunatic, distorted fashion.

He claimed the Jews also had financial motives, that they were promoting this worthless new work in order to drive down the value of Old Masters, which they then bought with the proceeds from the sale of the modern art. He felt assured of this last point after looking over the inventories of property seized from Jews, announcing with great satisfaction that the loot included many important paintings of the past.

In 1937, Hitler established the House of German Art in Munich for the exhibition of what he considered outstanding examples of "good German art," consisting almost exclusively of idealized representations of peasant life, hardy youth and heroic soldiers.

Among the benefits the new Museum offered, said Hitler, was that people who bought pictures here could be sure they were getting their money's worth. They would be freed from having to rely on their own judgment.

Reviewing the pictures to be hung in the opening exhibit, he discovered some he considered unfit. To make sure they were not included, he kicked holes in them. This was a minor episode compared to what lay in store for other paintings.

The Exhibition of Degenerate Art

After the Nazis came to power, they began purging German museums of anything they classified as "degenerate, Bolshevik and Jewish," ultimately confiscating about sixteen thousand such works, including pictures by Picasso, Van Gogh and Gauguin.

In conjunction with the opening of the House of German Art, Hitler ordered a separate exhibition, culled from the confiscated work. This show was heralded as a display of Degenerate Art, a reminder for right-thinking Germans of just what had been going on before the Nazi purge.

To make sure visitors got the point, the works were displayed in as chaotic a fashion as possible, with derisive captions such as "Thus Did Sick Minds View Nature." To compound the effect, the work of genuine mental patients, collected from asylums, was included.

The public poured in—some doubtless with hopes of seeing something bizarre, others probably suspecting this would be their last chance to see work they admired. Whatever their various reasons, over two million people visited during the four month run, making the Exhibition of Degenerate Art one of the most successful shows in history.

After the Exhibition, the Nazis sold many of the pictures outside the country, but not all were deemed worth putting up for sale. These, about four thousand works of art, were turned over to the Berlin fire department, which incinerated them in a ceremonial bonfire.

In art, as with almost everything he touched, Hitler's only significant accomplishment was destruction.

TWENTY-THREE

Hitler the Builder

How I wish I had been an architect.

—HITLER

Hitler's ideas about architecture were entirely consistent with his general ideology—simplistic, inhuman and cranky. He considered having all apartments standardized because variety in room shapes and sizes existed only to "give shopkeepers a chance of making more money . . . You change your apartment, and your curtains are no longer any use to you!"

Hitler saw plots and assault in everything, even in the shapes of roofs. Only slanted roofs, he declared, were properly Aryan because only this style was practical in a climate of rain and snow. Anyone who built a flat roof was succumbing to "Oriental, Semitic" influences.

Perhaps because of his rejection by the painting school of the Vienna Academy (see chapter 22, "The Art Dictator"), Hitler ultimately concluded that architecture was the greatest of the arts. Frequently, he bemoaned the fact that Destiny had called him to politics; otherwise, he maintained, he would have become a great architect.

This complaint, though, was often followed with the smug reflection that perhaps things had worked out best after all, because his success in politics had won him the power to commission vast projects and remodel the world to his design.

He had grandiose plans for the cities of the Reich but, characteristically, his methods were devious and he always kept a careful eye on public opinion. Wanting to tear down the Berlin Town Hall, a structure he happened to dislike, he launched a clandestine propaganda campaign, ordering anonymous letters written to the newspapers complaining about the old building. When these letters elicited unfavorable reader response, he decided to leave the Town Hall alone.

This small anecdote has chilling implications. Hitler had not become master of Germany by advocating unpopular causes. The Germans may have been led to catastrophic violence, but they were not pushed.

The Builder

When Hitler did build, it was on a massive scale, often deliberately oppressive. At the beginning of 1938, he told architect Albert Speer that he was planning a series of extremely important diplomatic conferences which would result in the reshaping of Europe. These conferences required an appropriate setting—a great new Chancellery. The building itself was to support his brutally aggressive foreign policy. He ordered Speer to build "grand halls and salons which will make an impression on people, especially the smaller dignitaries."

In less than a year, the new Chancellery was finished.

As ordered, it was vast and intimidating. The grand gallery leading to the principal reception room was twice the length of the Hall of Mirrors in Versailles. Hitler was delighted. Entering the room that would serve as his study, his eye caught a detail he recognized as epitomizing the whole undertaking. It was an inlay on his desk, showing a sword half drawn from its scabbard. "When the diplomats sitting in front of me see that," he said, "they'll learn to shiver and shake."

Even as Hitler built, his mind was on death and decay. He expected to be remembered by the monuments he left and worried how his palaces and stadiums would look as ruins a thousand years in the future. Speer obliged by using only those materials which would be dignified even in collapse. Steel girders, for example, were avoided wherever possible because they made for unsightly ruins.

This thinking did not save the new Chancellery from oblivion. It survived the war, but then the Russians demolished it and used the stone to build their principal war memorial in Berlin.

The Berghof and the Eagle's Nest

Hitler maintained a private estate in an idyllic mountain resort area near the Austrian border, just above the town of Berchtesgaden. His house there was originally a modest country cottage, but as his wealth and power grew, so did the cottage. Extensive expansion ultimately transformed it into a sprawling mansion called the Berghof (Mountain Hall).

Hitler himself drew the plans for much of the expansion, including the design for one of the Berghof's most spectacular features. This was an innovation—a huge picture window which despite its great size could be lowered completely out of the way, rather like a giant car window—to provide an open air view of the magnificent mountain scenery.

Although the mechanism worked perfectly, the window was rarely lowered because Hitler had miscalculated. The garage and motor pool were on the level immediately below the window so that when it was opened, the Berghof's great reception room was filled with the smell of gasoline.

A few miles from the Berghof, at the very top of Kehlstein peak, sat that legendary building known as the Eagle's Nest. To get to it, visitors entered a tunnel that led into the heart of the mountain, then boarded an elevator that carried them up the equivalent of thirty-five stories, into the Eagle's Nest.

Popular myth sometimes has this as Hitler's home. It was in fact little more than a reception room and a kitchen, but its location made it extraordinary. Circular, with windows on all sides, it provided a view so spectacular as to be disorienting. After a visit here, the French Ambassador, Francois-Poncet, described the Eagle's Nest as appearing "to be suspended in the void and almost hanging over it . . . bathed in the glow of an autumn evening, it is glamorous, wild, almost eerie. The visitor wonders whether he is awake or dreaming."

Hitler had nothing to do with designing Eagle's Nest but he had allowed a sycophantic underling, Martin Bormann, to build it for him at a cost of tens of millions of Marks. Twelve workmen were killed in the course of its construction. And in the end, Hitler visited it less than half a dozen times. According to one report, the height gave him heart palpitations and made him pant.

After World War II began, Hitler became less interested in houses and more concerned with bomb shelters. Wherever he spent time—at the Berghof, the Chancellery, or his various military headquarters, an elaborate shelter was always ready for him. Sometimes the entire headquarters was bombproof. The construction of one of these super-safe H.Q.'s (appropriately code-named "Giant") consumed more concrete than was allotted for the building of bomb shelters for the entire German population in 1944. As always, Hitler's first concern was for himself.

TWENTY-FOUR

Private Finances

All tax notices, so far as they would establish an obligation for the Fuehrer, are without legal effect.

—LUDWIG MIRRE,
PRESIDENT OF THE
STATE FINANCE OFFICE

The question of exactly when and why German big business began supporting Hitler is somewhat technical and remains a matter of controversy among historians. This chapter focuses on a subject which is not disputed—how Hitler handled his personal finances and the insight this provides about his character and methods.

Even when money was short, during the years of struggle to gain power, Hitler habitually left large tips in restaurants and hotels—three or four times the customary amount. Challenged by exasperated associates, he argued that this gave him celebrity status and thereby promoted the Nazi Party. Frequently, he added, he was asked to autograph the money, transforming the bills into valued souvenirs. Like any successful politician, he cultivated popular support at every opportunity.

Income

The bulk of Hitler's income was the ten percent royalty he received from the sales of *Mein Kampf*, his autobiographical manifesto (see chapter 3, "Hitler's Book").

Sales fluctuated in inverse proportion to the overall health of the German economy in the 1920s and early '30s. When times were good, sales of *Mein Kampf* lagged. When the economy faltered and people became desperate for solutions, interest in Hitler and his book climbed.

He also received generous payment for the frequent articles he wrote and required the Party's newspapers to publish.

As his fame increased, the foreign press began asking for interviews and articles. He was invited to say whatever he wanted about himself, the Nazi Party and Germany, and this propaganda was not only published, but paid for. The Hearst syndicate was a particularly good customer, giving him thousands of dollars per article.

Even at these rates, money was a secondary consideration. Hitler became furious on one occasion when he learned an aide had held up release of an article to the foreign press in an attempt to get better terms. He had wanted it published quickly because of the particular propaganda it contained.

Hitler as Taxpayer

Before he became Chancellor, Hitler raised money for regional Party organizations by speaking at rallies throughout the country. His pay for this was a cut of whatever was raised by the sale of tickets and contributions, but the exact amount of his fee was often arrived at only after acrimonious wrangling with local Nazi officials.

He also argued with the tax collector, claiming these speaking fees were not income, only reimbursement for expenses and therefore not taxable. Throughout his career, until he became Chancellor, he was in a running battle with the tax authorities over this and other issues.

Whenever possible, he hid income entirely. Because the Party's books were open to tax audit, any money moving from the Party to Hitler was traceable. Therefore, patrons desiring to support this exciting new political personality were encouraged to make their contributions to him directly. To facilitate this, Hitler's personal stationery carried his checking account number.

Hitler's difficulties with the tax office ended shortly after January 30, 1933, when the occupational designation "Writer" on his file was struck out and replaced with "Reich Chancellor."

Despite his various evasions through the preceding years, he was still listed as owing nearly half a million Marks in back taxes (about $125,000).

The simplest (and safest) course for the tax collectors would have been to ignore the debt, but appearances had to be preserved, so an abstruse legalism was concocted which came to a simple conclusion—Hitler was declared tax-exempt and his debt was canceled. Hitler personally reviewed the details of this ruling before giving it his solemn approval.

There was one subsequent, awkward incident. Despite

all that had gone on, the bureaucratic machinery generated a new tax bill and sent it to Hitler.

Back down through channels, from the Chancellery to the tax office, came an ominous inquiry. Hadn't this all been settled?

To make quite certain he would never again be troubled on their account, the shaken officials removed Hitler's mailing address plate from its place in the tray. As far as the tax office was concerned, Adolf Hitler no longer existed.

Kickbacks and Postage Stamps

Early in his career, Hitler granted photographer Heinrich Hoffmann an important monopoly. Only Hoffmann could take officially sanctioned photographs of him. This turned into a vastly lucrative enterprise for both men. Hitler's picture was displayed everywhere in Nazi Germany; reproduction fees poured in to Hoffmann, who shared them with Hitler.

Hitler also appeared on a wide variety of German postage stamps. Some show him as the Great Orator; others, as the austere War Leader. On one stamp, he strikes a moody pose as he visits his birthplace; on another, he bends to accept a birthday bouquet from a small child. There is nothing extraordinary about a nation's leader appearing on its stamps, but Hitler may well have been the only one who ever got paid for the honor.

He received only a fraction of a percent of each stamp's face value, but he was able to authorize as many stamps as he wanted. So many were produced that post-war stamp collectors found the ordinary economics of their hobby turned upside down. Usually, a stamp's value increases with the passage of time. Acting on this assumption immediately after the War, dealers in New York and London paid high prices for the sheets of unused Hitler stamps sent home by Allied servicemen. When it was realized, though, just how many stamps the royalty-minded Fuehrer had ordered, the price dropped sharply. To this day, Hitler issues are a commonplace philatelic item.

Grand Gestures

Shortly after taking office, Hitler renounced his salary as Chancellor. Told he could not do this, he donated the money to the families of Nazis and policemen killed in the political riots preceding his accession to power. This donation was given a great deal of publicity; no announcement was made when he resumed his salary in following years.

He did not, however, renounce his author's royalties from *Mein Kampf*. Indeed, shortly before he took office, they were raised from the conventional ten percent to fifteen. Sales were skyrocketing because the book had become required reading, or at least a necessary ornament, in every German house and office. Additionally, a law was passed requiring every city, town and village in the Reich to buy copies to give to each new married couple.

And there was yet another source of income—the "Adolf Hitler Endowment Fund of German Industry." This was collected from German industrialists who were benefiting from the Nazi building boom, with the rationale that it allowed them to show their gratitude to the Fuehrer who was making it all possible.

A Final Donation

At some point, Hitler began receiving a sack of cash as an annual birthday present "from the troops." On April 20, 1945, ten days before his suicide, he received the last of these. Hefting the sack, he thoughtfully observed that it didn't feel as heavy as in previous years.

Hitler's Will

Hours before killing himself, Hitler dictated a will leaving almost all his assets to the Nazi apparatus, asking that enough be set aside for the support of a few relatives and retainers.

With the collapse of Nazi Germany, the money held in bank accounts became effectively worthless. Hitler's estate included some property—an apartment in Munich, some paintings—but after the war, Hitler's will was declared invalid and his assets seized by the government because of his role as "an active Nazi."

TWENTY-FIVE

Mussolini, Stalin, Franco

The man is crazy!

—MUSSOLINI, AFTER HIS
FIRST MEETING WITH HITLER

In the early years of his career, Hitler was sometimes called the German Mussolini. Trying to follow in the Italian dictator's footsteps nearly got him killed.

The Duce had seized power in 1922 by leading his Blackshirts to Rome; when the Fuehrer tried to seize the Munich Town Hall with his Brownshirts in 1923, the police opened fire. Nineteen men died, and Hitler ended up in jail.

Released at the end of 1924, he continued building the Nazi Party and by 1926 was doing well enough to be invited to visit Mussolini in Italy. His associates, greatly excited by this recognition, were appalled when he refused to go. It was a trip he would not make, he said, until he could demonstrate that he too had power and means. "To impress Mussolini," said Hitler, "I would have to arrive with at least three automobiles. I just haven't got them yet."

The First Visit

Eight years later, in June 1934, after he had been ruler of Germany for a year and a half, Hitler finally went to Italy. As he emerged from his plane in a rumpled business suit, he was chagrined to be met by a Mussolini resplendent in a glittering, bemedalled uniform.

The three day visit was a disaster. Ill at ease, Hitler talked so much and so repetitiously that Mussolini later described him as a "gramophone with just seven records" and concluded he was a madman.

The Second Visit

More than three years passed before the two met again, this time in Germany. Hitler was now more powerful than he had been in 1934, and much more confident. But Mussolini had a few tricks left for putting the upstart Fuehrer in his place. As the two began the ceremonial inspection of the Honor Guard, Mussolini suddenly stepped out at a fast clip, forcing Hitler to trot after him.

There was much that was childish about the two most dangerous men in Europe. In the basement of his Chancellery, Hitler had a powerful toy cannon which he used to knock down wooden soldiers painted with the uniforms of France, England, Poland and Russia. The Russians were given leering, brutal faces.

Usually, no one but Hitler was permitted to play with this toy, but he invited Mussolini to fire it. Mussolini had a grand time and carefully noted the results of his marksmanship in the official record kept with the gun.

Eclipsing Mussolini

As Hitler became more powerful, his admiration for Mussolini turned to disdain and he entertained his intimates with a caricatured impersonation. Assuming Mussolini's grandiose widespread, hand-on-hip stance, Hitler thrust out his jaw and orated in nonsense Italian: "Macaroni bel canto telegrafica basta."

Dissatisfied with the great square in Berlin which bore his name, Hitler planned to build another and said he would rename the old one "Mussolini Platz." It was good enough for that.

Franco

In 1936, Hitler and Mussolini backed Franco's overthrow of democracy in Spain. (One of Germany's contributions was a hideous pioneering experiment—the obliteration of a city by air power, memorialized by Picasso in his horrific *Guernica*.) In 1940, Hitler traveled to the Spanish border for a return favor. He wanted Franco's cooperation in a plan to capture Gibraltar, the British fortress controlling the Western approach to the Mediterranean.

Hitler expected a brief meeting but Franco, seeing no advantage for him in Hitler's plan and much risk, raised a series of complex reservations. The meeting stretched on for the better part of nine hours until Franco achieved the extraordinary distinction of outlasting Hitler in a conversation. The Fuehrer finally had to accept that he could not have Gibraltar without an armed invasion of Spain, something he was not yet prepared to do.

Hitler later complained he would rather have three or four teeth pulled than subject himself to another meeting with Franco.

Stalin

Not all dictators were as shrewd as Franco in their dealings with Hitler. In August 1939, Josef Stalin signed the notorious treaty which split Poland between Germany and the Soviet Union, and triggered Word War II. He then began selling Germany vast quantities of raw materials.

When, less than two years later, Hitler attacked the Soviet Union, Stalin refused to believe the initial reports and ordered his forces to do nothing which might provoke the Germans.

Even after the Russians began to defend themselves effectively, Hitler continued to regard Stalin as a kind of colleague, with problems similar to his own and willing to resort to the same brutal solutions. "In his own way," said Hitler, "he is a hell of a fellow." He joked that after the Nazis won he would employ Stalin to run the country for him.

When he made these remarks, Hitler did not envision that his forces would meet a shattering, pivotal defeat at Stalingrad, the city named for the Russian dictator.

In the End

After Mussolini was arrested by rebellious former supporters in 1943, he was held in an evacuated hotel thought to be unassailable because of its mountaintop location.

Hitler ordered his ally rescued, and this was accomplished with a raid which must be termed masterful—Mussolini was flown off the mountain in a tiny two-seat airplane.

Hitler soon sent Mussolini back to Italy with instructions to resist the Allied advance. The next time Mussolini was captured, he was not treated to a gentle imprisonment but was shot by Italian partisans. His corpse was then hung upside down on a public street alongside that of his mistress.

As for the relationship between Hitler and Stalin, there is one final note. Despite his sure knowledge that Hitler was dead, Stalin insisted he had survived (see chapter 32, "Hitler's Corpse"). He suggested that Hitler might be hiding out in Spain, plotting a return to power. Stalin's motives are unclear but he may have had hopes of launching a joint Allied-Soviet invasion of Spain and overthrowing Franco. Nothing came of this, but Stalin's assertions contributed mightily to the enduring "Hitler Is Alive!" myth.

And as for Franco . . . he continued to cherish the memory of the Fuehrer and the Duce, keeping their pictures in a place of honor for ten years after their deaths. It was only in 1955, on the occasion of a visit by the President of the United States (the former Supreme Commander of Allied Forces in Europe) that he removed his pictures of Hitler and Mussolini and replaced them with a portrait of Eisenhower.

TWENTY-SIX

Hitler and the USA

What is America but millionaires, beauty queens, stupid records and Hollywood?

—HITLER, 1933

Two Myths and a Fact

Contrary to a popular legend, Hitler never owned property in the United States. This peculiar tale apparently arose from a 1940 transaction in which a German citizen named Gabriel Eberwein, acting through an American attorney, bought nearly 14,000 acres of undeveloped land in Cheyenne County, Colorado.

Four years later, the land was seized by the U.S. government under regulations affecting property belonging to enemy aliens. In someone's mind, somewhere along the line, this was transmuted into a seizure of land from Hitler, which would have meant that at one time Hitler had indeed owned land in America.

It is also untrue, contrary to another popular legend, that Hitler ever sued Alan Cranston, then a journalist and later the senior Senator from California (see chapter 3, *"Mein Kampf*, Hitler's Book").

It is a fact that Hitler's wartime special train was code-named *Amerika*. Brought into service just before the attack on Poland in 1939, its fifteen cars included anti-aircraft batteries, a conference car and complex communications equipment.

The special trains of high ranking officials were often given geographic code names; there is no record as to why *Amerika* in particular was chosen for Hitler. Even after he declared war on the United States on December 11, 1941, (see below), no one got around to changing the name (to *Brandenburg*) until the end of January 1943.

Hitler's Ideas About America

Hitler had a healthy respect for America's enormous industrial capacity and on more than one occasion said it was American intervention in 1917 that had doomed Germany in the First World War.

In the early 1920s, he had hopes of turning at least some of that American strength to his advantage. Contributions were solicited from wealthy Americans who seemed sympathetic, including Henry Ford, who may or may not have contributed (see chapter 6, "Henry Ford's Nazi Medal").

Money wasn't the only thing about America that intrigued Hitler. In 1924, he sent an associate, Kurt Ludecke, to investigate the possible usefulness of the Ku Klux Klan.

Ludecke studied the Klan, met with its leaders, and concluded that the Klan was not sufficiently well organized or ruthless enough to be a Nazi auxiliary.

Hitler continued to please himself with fantasies about the United States, envisioning a Nazi-supported uprising by the descendants of Germans, who would seize the country on his behalf. He did not see this as a remote future. "We shall soon have an S.A. [Storm Troop] in America," he said in 1933, and talked of the United States becoming Germany's greatest ally once the Nazis undertook overseas expansion.

Perhaps because of his general failure to enlist American support, Hitler finally decided it wasn't worth having. He said America was weak and rotten because of the presence there of Jews and other "inferior races," principally blacks. In his opinion, the defeat of the South in the Civil War had been a tragedy.

Keeping the U.S. Neutral

Hitler's behavior regarding the U.S. until December 11, 1941, is perfectly understandable. He went to considerable lengths to ensure that the country was not given any excuse whatsoever to enter the war against him.

The German press was ordered to refrain from criticizing the United States, President Roosevelt and even Mrs. Roosevelt, who was not infrequently a target of abuse and ridicule.

At sea, German submarines were directed to exercise extreme caution against attacking ships which might be American. Mistakes were inevitable. Several American merchant ships were torpedoed and there were a number of incidents in which U.S. warships attacked or were attacked by U-boats. Hitler's policy, though, remained consistent and clear throughout this period—the United States was to be kept neutral.

December 11, 1941

When the Japanese attacked Pearl Harbor, many feared American entry into the war in Europe would be indefinitely postponed. Germany, after all, had not attacked; Americans might choose to concentrate entirely on the Pacific struggle. On December 8, 1941, Congress declared war only on Japan.

Three days later, on December 11, Hitler resolved the situation with a typically dramatic gesture—he declared war on the United States.

His reasons can only be guessed at. The existing treaty with Japan required each country to support the other only in the event of attack. Japan, of course, had not been attacked by the United States.

Hitler had given the Japanese Ambassador assurances in conversation that Germany would stand by Japan in whatever fight she might find herself, but Hitler never felt bound by a promise.

It is possible he hoped his declaration of war against the U.S. would move the Japanese to return the favor by attacking the Soviet Union, which he had invaded six months earlier and which was proving an unexpectedly resistant adversary. Japan wisely refrained.

Some historians speculate Hitler simply could not bear to miss out on the opportunity to fight an "historic" global war; others argue he had an unconscious need to defeat himself.

The answer may be that he made a simple miscalculation, similar to Japan's mistake, which was that this would be an easy victory, that Americans would not fight.

A few weeks after declaring war, he said, "I'll never believe an American soldier can fight like a hero."

The Fight

In the early part of the war, German submarines did considerable damage to American shipping, sometimes within sight of the Eastern and Gulf coasts. However, another Hitler plan against the United States came to nothing: he ordered the building of giant bombers which would cross the Atlantic and raid New York.

Rambling on in one of his evening monologues, he explained to his entourage that skyscrapers were particularly vulnerable to air attack and that a *blitz* against Manhattan would be more devastating than the bombing of London. For some reason, he also believed it was impossible to build air raid shelters in New York. He didn't say why.

Some work was done on the giant transatlantic bombers, but none were ever finished.

A Final Fantasy

It is hard to believe even Hitler thought this was possible, but he told his mistress, Eva Braun, that after the war she could go to Hollywood in order to play herself when a movie was made of their life.

TWENTY-SEVEN

Hitler's Horoscope

What on earth have the stars got to do with me?

—HITLER

For the convenience of those interested in making astrological calculations: Adolf Hitler was born at 6:30 p.m. on April 20, 1889, in the Austrian town of Braunau am Inn, the latitude and longitude of which are 48 degrees 16'N, 13 degrees 02'E.

Hitler himself had generally little interest in astrology and when he did give it serious attention the consequences for the astrologers were lethal.

Contemporary rumor and subsequent legend depict him consulting the stargazers before making critical decisions. Although there is no known instance of this occurring, there are a number of reasons for the tales.

Hitler began his political career in 1919, and it was at this very time, in the dislocated, uncertain years following Germany's defeat in the First World War that all the occult arts enjoyed a raging general vogue.

Furthermore, throughout his career Hitler encouraged people to believe him different from ordinary men in some glamorous, mysterious way (see chapter 12, "William Patrick Hitler"). Given the man and the climate, then, it is not at all surprising he was thought to be an experimenter in magic, or at the very least to have a staff astrologer.

He could be easily flattered by being told of prominent historical figures whose birth date coincided with his own, but this was only a matter of idle, passing amusement.

There was a persistent rumor that early in his career he took public speaking lessons from Erik Jan Hanussen, a stage magician who was also an astrologer (see chapter 8, "Backstage Hitler") but even if this was so, it is unlikely he was interested in Hanussen's astrology. Hitler regarded his destiny as something only he understood; astrologers could not calculate it.

Some tried. In the summer of 1923, a well-known astrologer, Elsbeth Ebertin, predicted Hitler would someday lead a great uprising giving birth to a German Freedom Movement. When his aides reported this good news to Hitler, he shrugged it off as completely irrelevant and went on with his plans, which included the November 1923 uprising known as the Beer Hall Putsch. This episode ended with Hitler in jail and nearly wrecked the Nazi Party. In later years, Hitler occasionally joked about the Ebertin prediction.

Belief in a Hitler astrologer was not limited to Germany. After World War II began, British authorities were briefly taken in by an enterprising Hungarian emigre named Louis De Wohl, who managed to persuade them that he was personally acquainted with Hitler's astrologer and could therefore tell them what advice Hitler would be receiving.

By the time the British realized they were being hoaxed, De Wohl had wangled himself an office, a salary and a captain's uniform. He was subsequently set to useful work in a psychological warfare unit, helping to produce fake German astrology magazines. These contained dire predictions of German defeats, and were smuggled into Germany as part of an overall demoralization scheme.

It is well established that some of the highest ranking Nazis believed fervently in the occult sciences. Heinrich Himmler, head of the S.S., was a devotee and so was Rudolf Hess, the Deputy Fuehrer, nominally the second most important man in Germany. It was Hess's interest that eventually inflamed Hitler against astrologers and doomed many of them.

On May 10, 1941, Hess flew a plane to Scotland, parachuted out and demanded an appointment with British officials. Entirely on his own, he had come with a plan for ending the war, the essence of which was that Britain should just quit. The British found this absurd.

Hitler was shocked by Hess's escapade, and furious. Someone had to be blamed for getting a high ranking Nazi to embark on this embarrassing farce.

Hess's interest in astrology was well known, so in a sweep dubbed *Aktion Hess*, mass arrests were made of astrologers and other occultists throughout the country. The net was spread wide. Faith healers were included and, by inexorable Nazi logic, Christian Scientists.

In his diary, Propaganda Minister Goebbels noted with caustic satisfaction, "Oddly enough, not a single clairvoyant predicted that he would be arrested. A poor advertisement for their profession!" Goebbels may not have known that some of the arrested occultists were later put to work on exceedingly eccentric schemes concocted by Himmler (see chapter 35, "Heinrich Himmler").

Goebbels certainly could not have imagined that eventually he and Hitler would themselves turn to astrology for comfort. That bizarre moment arrived four years later, in April 1945.

As they sat in Hitler's underground bunker in Berlin, with the Russians and the Allies closing in, Goebbels read to Hitler from a biography of the eighteenth-century German king, Frederick the Great. Frederick, himself locked in a war with Russia, had been on the verge of surrender when a miracle occurred—the death of the Russian leader. This inspired Frederick to keep fighting, eventually defeating the Russians.

Discussing this incident somehow led Goebbels and Hitler to send for horoscopes from Himmler's files. Whether these already existed or were specially drawn up is not clear, but remarkably, they contained a number of predictions which had proved accurate—war in 1939, early Nazi victories, then the calamitous reversals. According to these same horoscopes, a miracle would occur in mid-April and Hitler would be saved.

A few days later a "miracle" did occur and it was similar to the one in Frederick's biography. President Roosevelt died. Surely, this was the turning point. Champagne was served. Hitler and Goebbels were in ecstasy.

Their euphoria quickly evaporated in the face of facts, and two and a half weeks later both committed suicide as Berlin fell to the Russians.

TWENTY-EIGHT

Hitler's Atomic Bomb

While you experts are worrying about how to win this war, here is our Postal Minister who brings us the solution.

—HITLER

If there was any prospect more horrifying than Hitler with an atomic bomb, it was Hitler with an atomic bomb and a long-range missile. He got the missile and might well have had the bomb. The difference lay in his attitudes toward the two projects.

The missile was the V-2 and although initially indifferent to it, he became immensely excited on seeing film of a successful flight in July 1943. This would give him the power to do something his Air Force could no longer accomplish—punish England. (The "V" in V-2 did not stand for Victory, but for Vengeance.) Hitler urged that the missile be refined and deployed as quickly as possible.

Its predecessor, the V-1 "buzz bomb," was little more than a pilotless airplane. The V-2 was something totally new. The progenitor of today's intercontinental ballistic missile, it was a rocket that touched the edge of space before plunging in on its target at well beyond the speed of sound. Its victims were denied even the warning whine that usually accompanies an incoming bomb. There was no defense against it.

London first came under attack by V-2s on the evening of September 8, 1944, when two fell on the city's outskirts. Although the psychological effect was considerable, it was quickly apparent that because of its limited payload, the V-2 was not an efficient way to wage war . . . and that frightened Allied experts. Underestimating the irrationality of Hitler's military policy, they wondered why the Germans were wasting their shrinking resources on this spectacular but ineffective weapon.

The conclusion many came to was chilling—perhaps these were only test flights. Perhaps the conventional warheads would soon be replaced with atom bombs. Scientists at the U.S. bomb development center in Los Alamos, New Mexico, tuned in the BBC several times a day on shortwave radio, to assure themselves London was still there.

It had, after all, been the work of German scientists just before the war which had frightened the United States and Britain into trying to build a bomb in the first place. (The British effort was subsequently absorbed into the American project.) The Germans had published experiments proving that an explosive release of atomic energy—indicated as a theoretical possibility by Einstein's relativity theories—was achievable reality.

Einstein himself and many other Jewish physicists had left Germany in the '30s but more than enough non-Jews, including Otto Hahn and Werner Heisenberg, remained to give the Nazis bomb-building potential.

However, they and many of their colleagues faced a problem common to dictatorships—the requirement that science be reconciled with ideology.

Their opponents included mediocre scientists who had advanced their careers through allegiance to the Nazi Party, while others were Nazis by genuine conviction. One of these latter, Philip Lenard, had actually joined the Party before Hitler and had always been a fervent supporter of the man who became the Fuehrer. Lenard had easy access to Hitler with his argument that Einstein's relativity was "Jewish science"—therefore, false and corrupt.

Nuclear physics is literally inconceivable without relativity. The non-fanatic scientists, anxious to get on with their work, scrambled to justify relativity by claiming it actually derived from the work of non-Jews who had preceded Einstein. They also spent countless hours writing nonsensical declarations like the one which piously asserted that the physical theory of relativity had nothing to do with a Jewish "world philosophy of relativity." For their efforts, many of these men—who were, after all, trying to build a bomb for Hitler—were dubbed White Jews.

Another, quite contradictory, factor which may have influenced Hitler against the bomb was his fear that it might work too well. When the atomic chain reaction was explained to him, someone in the group asked if the scientists were certain the chain reaction could be contained. Was there a chance the world might be consumed by a single atomic blast? The scientists admitted this was a possibility. Hitler, it is reported, was clearly unhappy at the prospect of the world he planned on ruling being turned into a fireball.

The physics underlying the V-2 were neither extraordinary nor controversial. It had been possible to develop it without much attention from Hitler; by the time he saw it, it worked. All he had to do was order large scale production and deployment. The bomb, on the other hand, was abstract; the road to it, uncertain. Men whose politics suited Hitler said it wasn't possible at all.

But no one was actually forbidden from working on an atomic bomb and as a result no less than three bomb projects were underway at the same time—one by the Army, another by the Ministry of Education and Science, and a third by the Post Office. Baron Manfred von Ardenne, a scientist who had not been included in either of the first two groups, had made a fascinating discovery—a research budget that was not being spent. As it happened, this was in the Post Office Department, and Von Ardenne quickly persuaded the Post Office Minister to commission a uranium development program under his direction.

The three projects competed in the worst sense, withholding information, resources and expertise from each other. In the United States, meanwhile, precisely the opposite was happening. The Manhattan Project was a massive, well coordinated effort in which many different and often conflicting ideas could be pursued at the same time, and results quickly compared. Erroneous paths could be abandoned before they became too costly while fruitful ones were pursued to success.

The chaotic German effort was entirely consistent with Hitler's overall organizational policies. Although the Nazi image was one of monolithic efficiency, Hitler throughout his career had always set subordinates against each other so that no man or agency would grow powerful enough to threaten him.

By late 1942, physicist Heisenberg confided to Armaments Minister Speer that a bomb could not be built in less than three or four years, and even this would be possible only with a maximum, coordinated effort. Soon after this conversation, Germany was cut off from its supplies of tungsten, a metal used as the core for certain types of conventional ammunition. The tungsten could be replaced with uranium, and although uranium was essential to any nuclear project, it was now clear that an atomic bomb was not going to be built. Speer ordered the uranium diverted.

The German project was over in fact, but it lived on in Hitler's mind. As his empire collapsed with accelerating swiftness and reality became increasingly unacceptable, he hoped for a "miracle weapon" that would turn everything to his favor. An atomic bomb would be perfect. Fortunately, he came to this realization far too late to do anything effective about it and a Nazi atomic bomb remained nothing more than a comforting self-delusion. In February 1945, Hitler said in conversation that "the problem of nuclear fission was solved long ago and development has now reached the stage when we can put the resulting energy to military use. That will knock them into the middle of next week."

As part of this final, lunatic grasping at scientific straws, nuclear physicists were rounded up by the Gestapo, loaded on trucks along with lab equipment and taken to the mountains in the south, where a last stand was planned. This enterprise came to nothing and a world which had been spared little was at least spared an atomic bomb in Hitler's hands.

TWENTY-NINE

The Olympic Patron

*In physique and general appearance the boys
and girls of Germany and Italy are now the finest
in Europe.*

—G. WARD PRICE,
ENGLISH JOURNALIST

Hitler is generally given far more credit than he deserves for the great propaganda success which the 1936 Olympics scored for him and Nazi Germany. He was slow to recognize there might be any value in them at all, and even then his obstinacy and prejudices nearly wrecked the undertaking.

In 1932, when the International Olympic Committee selected Germany as the Host for 1936, Hitler denounced the Games as "an invention of Jews and Freemasons" which "could not possibly be put on in a Reich ruled by National Socialists." At that time, Germany was not ruled by the Nazis; that calamity did not come to pass until the beginning of 1933.

The Olympic Committee's choice had symbolic significance. Berlin had been the designated site for the 1916 Games, never held because of the First World War.

Thereafter, as punishment for its aggressor role, Germany was not allowed to even enter the Olympics until 1928. The awarding of the 1936 Games—a decision made while Germany was still a democracy—was supposed to acknowledge the nation's rehabilitation.

In 1933, Hitler came to power but despite his earlier stand, he did not oppose the Games. Indeed, he welcomed them, though he seemed excited principally by the architectural prospects they offered. "If Germany is to stand host to the entire world," he said, "her preparations must be complete and magnificent." A massive building program began.

The Olympics program aside, almost everything Hitler was doing frightened and depressed the world. By 1935, most particularly in the United States but elsewhere as well, people were demanding the Games be moved or boycotted. The most consistently disturbing news was the persecution of Jews; increasingly, the question was asked—would there be any Jews on Germany's teams? The answer seemed to be no.

To calm the uproar this prospect was causing, the Nazis announced that German Jews could participate . . . if they could qualify. Of course, by 1935, Jews had been thrown out of all German sports clubs and denied the right to form their own. And organized or not, they were forbidden to use all recreational areas, including—but not limited to—playing fields, ski slopes, swimming pools and beaches.

But if the world demanded Jews on the German teams, Jews would be found. Ultimately, one was chosen for the Winter games, one for the Summer. Both had to be recruited from aboard, having already emigrated.

In preparation for the Games, as part of the effort to hide the evil unfolding in Germany, public displays of anti-Semitism were ordered toned down. There were to be no beatings, no riots, no public humiliations. The commonplace roadside signs such as "The Jews Are Our Misfortune" and "It is dangerous for Jews to enter this town" and simply "Death to Jews Here" were to be removed.

The cleanup order wasn't much obeyed; the head of the International Olympic Committee, Count Baillet-Latour, met with Hitler and demanded the hate signs be removed. Hitler refused, saying that "a small point of Olympic protocol" did not warrant interference with the feelings of the German people. Baillet-Latour thereupon threatened to cancel the Games.

Hitler talked on a few more moments about Germany's problems, then lapsed into a silence lasting for minutes. Baillet-Latour waited. Finally, Hitler announced, "You will be satisfied; the orders shall be given" and abruptly left the room. The signs quickly disappeared.

By this time, Hitler had realized the Olympics were a superb public relations opportunity, a chance to show the world that Germany was a happy country and that he was a peaceful man. However, despite the pleas of associates that he appear at the Olympics in civilian dress, he was adamant about wearing his military style Nazi Party uniform. He also had himself named "patron and protector" of the Games, an unprecedented appointment which has not been repeated.

Hitler had nothing to do with two innovations which have remained a permanent part of the Olympics. The

Berlin Games were the first ever televised, although the image quality was so poor only the most imaginative optimist could have imagined television's future importance. The other innovation was an immediate and unqualified success—the carrying of the Olympic flame from Greece to the site of the modern Games.

Olympic custom allows the host nation a noncompetitive exhibition sport. The Germans made a choice of ominous significance, evidently feeling no qualms about demonstrating their achievements in gliding. (The treaty ending the First World War forbade a German Air Force; gliding was proving an effective way of circumventing the restriction so that future combat pilots could be trained.)

At the Games, Hitler was a profoundly involved spectator, jiggling his legs in excitement, gripping the edge of his box, often rising to his feet. Sport as such did not much interest him, but this was Germany against the world. One observer noted that to Hitler each event "was a war in which the Fatherland had to win . . . if a German won, he relaxed and smiled all over his face; if a German lost, he scowled."

Hitler was made particularly unhappy by the performance of Cornelius "Corny" Johnson, who won a gold medal in the high jump. Johnson was an American but his great offense was that he was black. His victory caused Hitler to abandon publicly congratulating winners; German victors were rewarded with private audiences.

It was, of course, another black American, Jesse Owens, who seized the world's attention with his spectacular achievements in Berlin. Even the Germans were wildly enthusiastic about him.

One of Hitler's advisers suggested he meet Owens, saying this would have a wonderful effect on world opinion. Enraged by the very thought, Hitler shouted, "Do you really think that I will allow myself to be photographed shaking hands with a Negro?"

Hitler's convictions were impervious to facts; his belief in the superiority of the white man was not in the least disturbed by the achievements of Owens, Johnson, and other black athletes. He concluded that their performance only proved they were closer to animals than to men. They should be described, he said, not as team members but as "black auxiliaries" and, "The Americans ought to be ashamed of themselves for letting their medals be won by Negroes."

Despite Hitler's attitude, he scored an enormous propaganda victory with the Olympics. For one thing, Germany won more medals than any other nation. The United States came in second but Italy was third and Japan beat Great Britain. Overall, the dictatorships did much better than the democracies, a fact much discussed on both sides.

Furthermore, again despite the Fuehrer's occasional lapses, the national charade succeeded beautifully. The world saw a prospering, cheerful Germany with no evidence of the regime's grinding brutality against its opponents or the internal war against the Jews.

Hitler meanwhile had incorporated the Olympics into his dream of world conquest, instructing architect Albert Speer to build a mammoth new sports stadium which would accommodate 400,000 spectators.

As the two reviewed a model of the new stadium, Speer pointed out the planned athletic field did not conform to Olympic specifications. Hitler said that did not matter. In the future, the Olympic Games would take place nowhere else but Germany "for all time to come" and then of course, "we will determine the measurements."

Hitler did allow that the next Games could take place as planned; after all, the Host chosen by the International Olympic Committee was an ally. The 1940 Games were scheduled for Tokyo.

THIRTY

Why Didn't Somebody
Kill Him?

*. . . there are thousands of Germans who would
kill their Fuehrer if they had a chance and pay
the penalty with their own lives. At least this is
common talk in indirect ways.*

—WILLIAM E. DODD,
U.S. AMBASSADOR,
APRIL 1935

Nearly a dozen attempts were made on Hitler's life
between the time he became Chancellor in 1933
and the beginning of World War II. He derided the
would-be assassins, saying had they been idealists willing to risk their own lives, they would probably have
succeeded. This was untrue. Hitler protected himself
very carefully.

He gave bulletproof limousines as Christmas presents
to his closest associates and always used them himself.
During parades he often stood in open cars, but was
likely to be wearing a bulletproof vest and a steel lined
cap (see chapter 16, "Hitler's Wardrobe"). He certainly
took other security precautions, the most obvious of

which were the ranks of guards protecting him during parades and speeches.

Regulations abounded. Aides often appeared with baskets of rose petals for the crowd to strew in Hitler's path, but a law forbade throwing a bouquet at him. It might contain a bomb.

Although all the prewar attempts failed without so much as a shot being fired, the Fuehrer's justice was harsh. At least six of the would-be assassins were beheaded.

The Elser Attempt

Hitler's habit of making last minute changes in his schedule was more a matter of personal inclination than a deliberate attempt to thwart would-be assassins, but it did make attempts on his life all the more difficult to plan.

It was, however, always certain where he would be between 8:30 and 10 p.m. each November 8th. This was the anniversary of his 1923 attempt to seize power, which began in a Munich beer hall and ended the next day in a hail of police bullets.

Each November 8th, Hitler returned to the beer hall and gave a speech, invariably beginning at 8:30 and talking until at least ten. On November 8th, 1939, he began half an hour early, was uncharacteristically brief, and was finished and out of the hall by 9:07.

Thirteen minutes later, a tremendous explosion shattered the pillar immediately behind the rostrum, bringing down part of the roof. Dozens were killed and wounded.

Had Hitler still been there, he would have been blown to pieces.

Throughout his career Hitler claimed divine guidance and protection. Because he had so narrowly missed being killed on this occasion, a story quickly arose that this had been a phony attempt, set up by Hitler himself to prove his invulnerability.

Within hours after the bombing, the police arrested a Swiss cabinetmaker, Georg Elser, as he tried to cross the border back to Switzerland. He was carrying a picture postcard of the beer hall, technical data about explosives, and parts of a bomb detonator.

Elser admitted the bombing. Indeed, he claimed sole responsibility for it, saying that he had circumvented the tightened security preceding Hitler's appearance by planting the bomb two and a half days before the speech. If that were true, the bomb's mechanism must have been ingeniously complex.

Speculating that it was impossible for a lone assassin to have accomplished all this, some concluded the attempt was real enough and that it was organized by rivals of Hitler within the Nazi Party.

Hitler himself decided—without any supporting evidence whatsoever—that Elser was part of a conspiracy undertaken by British Intelligence agents. He wanted the agents caught and put on public trial, believing this would gravely discredit the British government.

In prison, Elser stuck to his story of having worked alone, despite interrogations which included hypnosis, drugs and beatings. Given the materials he called for, he was able to make a duplicate of the bomb's complex timing mechanism.

Hitler's obstinate insistence on being proved correct nearly saved Elser's life. Once the interrogations were over, everything was done to keep this important prisoner healthy and reasonably contented; he was, after all, to be the star witness in the trial of the British agents . . . whenever they were rounded up. As the years passed, despite having a great deal else on his mind, Hitler would occasionally bring the matter up to Himmler, head of the S.S., goading him about his failure to establish the British involvement.

It was not until April 1945, that Elser was murdered by the S.S. and his death reported as an air-raid casualty. The reason for the killing and the cover-up are not known.

German Army Attempts

Hitler's taunt that he could be killed by any assassin willing to sacrifice his own life was true enough for those who could get close to him, including high-ranking military personnel. As his foreign policy grew more recklessly aggressive in the late 1930s, some Army officers, fearing he would trigger a general European war they were not sure they could win, began to brood and even lay plans for arresting Hitler or killing him.

He was saved, in large part, by Western diplomacy. A serious Army plot against him began to take shape as he prepared to attack Czechoslovakia, but when Britain and France backed down and allowed him his easy conquest, Hitler's popularity soared. The plotters abandoned their plan, reckoning that a coup would find little support among their colleagues or the public.

The first phase of World War II only enhanced Hitler's popularity; the collapse of France in June 1940 marked the apogee of his reputation. Within a year and a half, however, he had Germany firmly on the road to cataclysmic defeat . . . and Army assassination plots against him began to multiply. Some were elaborate and serious; others may have been exaggerated in the postwar telling.

Various officers on various occasions carried bombs and pistols into his presence but somehow never used them. One bomb placed aboard his plane simply failed to go off although the fuse and detonator worked.

Colonel Claus von Stauffenberg came closest to killing Hitler. While recovering from severe wounds suffered in combat in April 1943, Stauffenberg decided God had spared his life so he could perform a noble deed. The assassination of Hitler, he believed, would mean the collapse of the Nazi government, and that might persuade the Allies to end the war without the invasion and defeat of Germany, a prospect which seemed otherwise inevitable. Already acquainted with other potential conspirators in high places, Stauffenberg ultimately managed to get himself appointed to a position which gave him the opportunity of meeting personally with Hitler.

On July 20, 1944, he was summoned to Hitler's military headquarters in East Prussia to deliver a report. When he entered the conference room, he carried a briefcase with the report and a bomb set to explode in ten minutes. A discussion was in progress when he arrived; maps covered the heavy oak table.

Seeing that his report was not expected immediately, Stauffenberg put down his briefcase and excused himself from the room, saying he was expecting a telephone call from Berlin with last minute data.

He went to his car and waited. Shortly thereafter, there was a terrific blast, smoke, then casualties being carried from the building.

Stauffenberg immediately headed for the nearby airfield, where he boarded a plane for Berlin; Hitler's death was supposed to set an elaborate and thorough coup in motion.

Hitler was not dead. The blast had killed and wounded many in the room; but moments before the explosion, an officer stepping closer to Hitler, finding the briefcase in his way, had pushed it with his foot . . . under the heavy conference table.

Hitler had been shielded from the blast's full force. His hair was singed, his eardrums damaged, his right arm badly bruised, but he was alive and functioning. Indeed, he was euphoric—his survival confirmed his belief he was protected by Providence. "I am invulnerable," he said over and over. "I am immortal."

When it became known Hitler had survived, the Army coup collapsed. Stauffenberg was arrested and shot that night. Others did not get off so easily. After abusive show trials, they were executed, some by hanging. These deaths were prolonged. Instead of having their necks broken by an abrupt drop, they were carefully lowered so they would slowly strangle. Their death agonies were filmed for Hitler and he had the film run repeatedly.

Allied Attempts

Where, it might well be asked, were the Allies in all this? Why did they not try to kill Hitler?

Once the war began, Hitler made few public appearances, staying generally close to his bombproof headquarters (see chapter 23, "Hitler the Builder"). It was expected he would preside at a parade in Paris celebrating the fall of France, and the British considered an attempt at assassination by air raid. Incredibly, this was finally ruled out on the grounds that such an attack would be improper and uncivilized. (In any event, Hitler did not attend the parade, precisely because of a concern the British might try to get him.)

On another occasion, Churchill rejected a similar attempt by saying this "would be like anarchy."

When British bombers did hit Hitler's mountain home, the Berghof, on April 25, 1945, the raid only underscored the futility of such attacks. The building was badly damaged but Hitler was in Berlin, hundreds of miles to the north. Had he been at the Berghof, he doubtless would have survived the raid in the extensive network of bomb shelters and tunnels dug deep into the rock beneath the house.

"What if . . ." is a favorite game for history buffs and "What if Hitler had been killed" is a fascinating prospect. But "What if . . ." is not a game played only after the fact. We now know that as long as he lived—but only for so long—the war and the Holocaust would continue. This was not clear at the time. A report prepared by the U.S. Office of Strategic Services in 1943 suggested that Hitler's death by assassination would only strengthen his post-war reputation among the Germans, making him a martyr and giving him a heroic stature. The situation would be even worse, says the report, if the assassin were Jewish because this undoubtedly "would be followed by the complete extermination of all Jews in Germany and the occupied countries." Of course by then, the Final Solution was fully systematized and industrialized, with Jews being murdered at the rate of thousands a day.

At the time, it was impossible to imagine just how much good the death of Adolf Hitler would accomplish.

THIRTY-ONE

Was Hitler Really Anti-Semitic?

*He then shouts, "Death to the Jews" etc. and
etc. There was frantic cheering. I never saw
such a sight in my life.*

—CAPT. TRUMAN SMITH,
U.S. MILITARY ATTACHE,
REPORTING ON A HITLER
SPEECH, 1922

Because he was cynical and duplicitous about so much, a perverse legend sometimes circulates that Hitler's anti-Semitism was little more than a position taken for political convenience. It is true that anti-Semitism was generally popular and therefore eminently serviceable as a Nazi rallying point, and on at least one occasion Hitler admitted that had there been no Jews, it would have been necessary to invent them. "It is essential," he said, "to have a tangible enemy, not merely an abstract one."

But this political observation must not obscure the fact that Hitler's hatred of Jews was genuine and so great as to be a defining characteristic of his personality. It was present in him early. A boyhood friend later recalled him at the age of fifteen complaining about Jews as an alien influence.

There is no mystery as to where Hitler picked up his anti-Semitism. This particular form of hatred has a long history in Central Europe, with Jews as the traditional scapegoat for calamity of every kind—pestilence, economic collapse, military defeat. Moreover, and of more specific significance, late in the nineteenth century an influential school of thought developed that sought to define a racial basis for the German nation. If the Germans were a separate and superior race, then—so went the argument—there had to be an abysmally inferior race. One could not be defined without the other; thus, degradation of Jews (including German Jews) became an integral part of German self-identification.

This pervasive anti-Semitism suited Hitler on a personal level, for even as a youth he needed someone to hate. The original cause of his anger—an early psychological trauma, perhaps a genetic predisposition—will never be known, but the course of his anti-Semitism can be tracked from a generalizing attitude to political policy and then to mass murder. On the other hand, some specific biographical causes for his anti-Semitism, as attributed by common legend, can be discarded.

It is true his mother died of cancer, despite a prolonged and very painful treatment administered by a Jewish physician, Dr. Eduard Bloch. But Hitler did not blame Bloch. On the contrary, he thanked him repeatedly for his efforts, and thirty years later Nazi authorities were ordered to go more easily on Bloch than was usually the case for Jews. Eventually, he was allowed to emigrate to the United States, although he had to leave almost all his savings behind.

Hitler evidently did blame Jews for his not being allowed to enter the Vienna Fine Art Academy (see chapter 22, "The Art Dictator"). Years later, when he was in power, he cracked a macabre joke—he was sure the Jews were sorry now they hadn't let him pursue a career as a painter or architect.

At the time, though, he was more than content with the Jewish art dealers to whom he peddled his watercolors. He preferred them, he said, to the Christians because the latter would buy only what they could sell quickly while the Jews were willing to take chances and stockpile.

He had Jewish friends in Vienna; frequently, he debated the question of Zionism with one of them. A reliable memoir reports him visiting synagogues, once taking a non-Jewish friend to observe a wedding. He knew enough about Jewish custom to explain that they were not to remove their hats here.

Despite this human contact, Hitler's anti-Semitic obsession grew. He delved into crackpot literature on the subject (see chapter 17, "Hitler's Bookshelf") and in the summer of 1908 made his first political commitment by joining a group called—baldly—The Anti-Semite Union.

From Vienna, he moved to Munich, where he enlisted when the First World War broke out. Unlike his fellow soldiers, who soon grew to hate the war, he found purpose and contentment in it (see chapter 10, "Hitler in Combat"); German surrender in November 1918 was a shattering personal trauma for which someone had to be blamed. It was, in Hitler's mind, the fault of the Jews, a sentiment which was to find enthusiastic reception throughout postwar, defeated Germany.

A year later, in September 1919, while working in the Army's political education office, Hitler was asked to prepare a position paper on the "Jewish question." In this document, the first known writing by him on the subject, he argues that one must not be emotionally anti-Semitic, but rationally so. Emotion, he says, leads to nothing more productive than occasional riots. Only a rational approach will result in a sustained struggle culminating in "the total removal of all Jews from our midst."

A month after writing his report, Hitler joined the obscure political club that was to become the Nazi Party. In the years following, specific points in the declared Nazi program changed, disappeared, resurfaced. One thing never changed—the Jews were to be destroyed.

The Nazis were bitter enemies of Communism, but Hitler acknowledged that a Communist could change his views and even become a loyal Nazi. Jews, however, would always be Jews. Religious conversion did not change their race, their apartness.

No single source more thoroughly demonstrates how completely entwined anti-Semitism was with Hitler's views of culture, history and politics than his autobiography-manifesto, *Mein Kampf*. According to it, Jews have been waging a war throughout history against all that is decent and vigorous; there is no fault for which they are not ultimately responsible, including syphilis. His argument is laced with lurid sexual imagery. Jews are depicted as poisoning Gentile bloodlines through rape.

Historians have tried to determine whether Hitler's murder of millions of Jews in the Holocaust was merely the fulfillment of one part of a plan for world conquest, or had all along been his principal goal, *the* motive for acquiring power. Whatever the answer, there seems no doubt mass murder was always high on the agenda. In 1922, Hitler told an associate, "Once I am really in power, my first and foremost task will be the annihilation of the Jews."

Throughout the 1920s and into the '30s, he hammered away, building his Party, accumulating popular support throughout the country. In his speeches, whatever the immediate issue at hand, the Jews are almost always the ultimate source of the trouble.

Hitler was the consummate dissembler, capable of many poses, but all observers agree that to see him unleashing his hatred for Jews, to see him barking his threats, this was to see truly into the spitting cauldron of his soul. And these displays were not limited to the public platform. In instance after instance, at a dinner table or in casual conversation, if someone mentioned the word "Jew," Hitler instantly plunged into a near trancelike state, raging furiously for up to half an hour until abruptly the storm passed and he resumed a more ordinary tone.

To Hitler, "Jew" had become a vivid synonym for all that was detestable, for anything which opposed or restrained him. He said, "Conscience is a Jewish invention. It is a blemish, like circumcision."

Other revolutions in history have been marked by crowds toppling the statues of kings or the freeing of political prisoners. The so-called Brown Revolution—

Hitler's becoming Chancellor in January 1933—was celebrated by days of nationwide anti-Jewish riots. Hitler quite literally laughed in delight when given reports of violence and indignities committed against Jews.

In a cynical parody of civilized procedure, the Nazi government, often with Hitler's personal participation, now formulated a systematic series of anti-Semitic laws. The Law Against the Overcrowding of German Schools, for example, effectively denied Jews the opportunity of higher education, while another established a Reich Chamber of Culture which ejected Jews from the entertainment and arts professions. In time, German Jews were barred from every aspect of German life . . . but there was no single sudden shock. Jews, and world opinion, were kept off balance, wondering just how far this would go. In response to complaints within the Nazi Party that he was not moving against the Jews quickly enough, Hitler said, "You must understand that I always go as far as I dare and never further. It is vital to have a sixth sense that tells you, broadly, what you can do and what you cannot do."

On September 15, 1935, Hitler capped the festivities of the annual Nuremberg Party Day with the announcement of the notorious "Nuremberg Laws," which were concise and comprehensive. Marriage was forbidden between Jews and non-Jews, and all Jews were stripped of their German citizenship. The assault relented during most of 1936 as part of the national charade for the Olympics (see chapter 28, "The Olympic Patron") but thereafter the baiting, beatings and arrests resumed in full force.

Jewish property was seized in a variety of ingenious

ways. Perhaps the single most grotesque instance was the penalty levied after the November 1938 pogrom which became known as "Crystal Night" for all the shattered glass it produced. Synagogues were razed, Jewish owned stores pillaged; there were countless beatings and outrages, and nearly a hundred Jews were killed outright. Hitler thereupon decreed that the Jewish community would have to pay a fee to the State in recompense for the ravages and disruptions of Crystal Night. This was assessed at one billion marks, approximately 250 million dollars.

As Hitler seized neighboring countries, first by political maneuver and then by war, the Jews in these countries also became his victims. The scope of the massive atrocities which were undertaken cannot be adequately described in this brief essay. At Hitler's direction, the resources of a victorious military power were directed against helpless men, women and children. Six million people were murdered.

Shortly after coming to power, Hitler had established concentration camps to imprison and torture his opponents. Prisoners were sometimes released from these, but in the late '30s they were considerably enlarged to accommodate tens of thousands of German Jewish prisoners who were worked and starved to death.

After the invasion of Poland and then the Soviet Union, as the Germans advanced, Jews were simply lined up and shot, but this was deemed inefficient and soon murder by gassing began, using mobile units. By June 1942, vast new camps, the most murderous of which was the Auschwitz complex, were in operation, built specifically to serve as death factories. Jews were rounded up throughout Germany and all of Nazi occupied Europe, in implementation of the euphemistically named Final Solution. Hitler meant to kill every Jew in Europe.

Knowing that to threaten Jews in speeches was one thing while mass murder would tarnish his image as a great and good man, he went to considerable lengths to hide these murders and in particular his connection with them. In this matter, he issued only verbal orders.

Overall, the mass murder program which the world remembers as the Holocaust was kept as secret as possible. Had Hitler succeeded in his war on the world, had there been no war crimes trials, knowledge of the Holocaust might well have vanished completely by now.

As it was, as his Empire collapsed and his death camps fell into the hands of the Russians and the Allies, Hitler raged, not because his crimes were uncovered but because the prisoners were being left behind by fleeing guards. He wanted them evacuated so they could be murdered at camps still in Nazi hands.

Finally, in the hours before his suicide, with much of Europe in ruins and tens of millions dead as the direct result of his obsessions and ambitions, Hitler dictated "My Political Testament," in which he blames the Second World War on Jews, saying he never wanted it and that it was "desired and instigated exclusively by those international statesmen who were either of Jewish origin or working for Jewish interests."

Hitler closes his Testament with a charge to those who will survive. They are to maintain "a merciless resistance against the poisoners of all peoples, international Jewry." This final message of hate is Hitler's legacy, the sum total and culmination of his career.

THIRTY-TWO

Hitler's Corpse

That snake Hitler is dead. He shot himself, and they burned his corpse. We found his charred carcass.

—MARSHAL G. K. ZHUKOV,
RED ARMY COMMANDER,
MAY 1945

Despite decades of stories about Hitler "alive and well and living in . . . ," the established facts are: Some time after 3:30 in the afternoon of April 30, 1945, Hitler and Eva Braun, whom he had married a day and a half earlier, entered Hitler's private suite in his Chancellery bunker and there committed suicide. As Hitler had ordered, their bodies were then carried out of the bunker into what remained of the Chancellery garden, where gasoline was poured on them and ignited. The cremation proved inadequate; the remains were substantial. That night, the charred corpses were moved to a shell crater and buried.

All this was determined through investigations conducted by American and British authorities. Dozens of participants and witnesses were questioned repeatedly

and their accounts carefully cross-checked. One reason
for the extraordinary thoroughness of the investigations
was that a determined effort to obscure the facts had
been made—not by the Nazis, but by the Russians.

Berlin had fallen to the Red Army; the Russians were
the first to enter the Chancellery, and they repeatedly
asserted they had found Hitler's remains. Then, on June
9, more than a month after finding the bodies, the Russians changed their story. They called a press conference, to announce their belief that Hitler and his wife
had escaped Berlin. On July 17, Stalin personally repeated this to President Truman at the Potsdam Conference, adding that he thought Hitler was now in Spain or
Argentina.

It is unlikely we will ever know just what Stalin had
in mind—a genuine if irrational conviction, or the hope
of exploiting "Hitler alive" for specific ends. Mentioning
the possibility that Hitler was in Spain, for example, may
have been a way of sounding out the western Allies on
the possibility of an overthrow of Franco.

To assure his lie's success, Stalin suppressed a considerable body of evidence. The Allies offered to share
data but the Russians refused any cooperation or
exchange.

Among other things, they had found Hitler's dental
records, invaluable in establishing post-mortem identification. They took most of the witnesses who had fallen
into their hands back to Russia—including Hitler's valet
and his personal adjutant, both of whom had helped dis-
pose of the bodies. These men and others survived, and
when released in 1955 the information they supplied
confirmed the account already established by the West.

Then, in 1968—twenty-three years after Hitler's death—the Russians allowed publication of an extraordinary book, *The Death of Adolf Hitler*. Its contents include a Hitler autopsy report, a photograph of charred and decomposed remains, and photograph of teeth and dentures purportedly removed from the remains. The book admits Stalin lied. As his motive, it gives the somewhat unlikely explanation that if a Hitler imposter turned up claiming to have been saved by a miracle, Stalin wanted to be able to refute the imposter with proof of Hitler's death.

But if the Russians had lied before, and given this explanation of Stalin's motive, could they be believed now? *The Death of Adolf Hitler* is clearly a Cold War document with an agenda beyond the reporting of ascertainable physical facts. Reviewing Hitler's career, for example, it claims a similarity between his aims and the policies of NATO, the postwar Allied security pact.

The book says Hitler died solely from cyanide poisoning, lacking the "manly" resolve necessary to shoot himself. In fact, the mass of evidence suggests Hitler managed to simultaneously bite down on a cyanide capsule and shoot himself.

It was also held against the reliability of *The Death of Adolf Hitler* that it did not answer the question raised by the very fact of its being published at all—why now?

Although he was never able to penetrate the motives of the Russians, Dr. Reidar Sognnaes, Dean of the UCLA School of Dentistry, was exactly the right man to examine the validity of the Russian autopsy. An expert in the identification of bodies through dental evidence, his hobby was studying the teeth of famous historical figures.

Sognnaes recalled reading that Hitler's dentist had supplied Allied investigators with detailed testimony on Hitler's teeth and dentures (see chapter 15, "I Was Hitler's Dentist"). He found the interrogation report in U.S. archives and also tracked down X rays that had been made of Hitler's skull and jaws as part of an examination following the July 20, 1944, bomb assassination attempt (see chapter 29, "Why Didn't Somebody Kill Him?").

Using the notes and the X rays, Sognnaes made an exhaustive comparison with the Russian evidence and concluded the Russian had indeed found and correctly identified Hitler's corpse shortly after his death in 1945. Although disputes on this still flare up from time to time, Sognnaes's report is generally accepted as conclusive.

As to the final disposition of Hitler's remains—the Russians report that after the autopsy, his corpse was burned to ashes and scattered to the wind.

Had the Russians released their report in 1945 instead of 1968, the world might have been spared the countless stories of Hitler seen boarding giant U-boats taking him to Argentina or the Arctic, working as a waiter in a Bavarian hotel, etc. But perhaps not.

Popular imagination operates independently of facts and even now, when he would be over a hundred, "Hitler alive" stories endure, often in the form of Hitler revived or Hitler clones. It might be said the public needs Hitler alive because only a live Hitler can be punished, but in fact the legends dwell on Hitler alive, not Hitler punished.

It simply may be that a story requires an end befitting

it. Hitler plunged the world into cataclysmic events of a scale unprecedented in history. World War II was his war; the Holocaust was his creation. No man has ever been responsible for more misery. The story is unresolved if at the end all we have is a charred corpse and a technical treatise on dental identification.

Perhaps this is a very good thing. Hitler's career ought not to be perceived as a dramatic story with a satisfying conclusion, as though it were fiction.

THIRTY-THREE

Hermann Goering

*We are all creatures of the Fuehrer. His faith
makes us the most powerful of men.*

—GOERING

Hermann Goering was the fat one, most famous for
heading the *Luftwaffe*, the German air force. His
flamboyant cheerfulness and comic opera antics only
made him more dangerous, for they led both Germans
and foreigners to underestimate his efficient brutality. He
was in fact the principal administrator of some of Hitler's most murderous undertakings and said, "I have no
conscience. My conscience is Adolf Hitler."

A World War I flying ace, his war hero status alone
made him a valuable recruit when he joined the Nazis
in 1922, but he was also a ruthless bully and ferocious
nationalist. Hitler soon appointed him head of the S.A.,
the brownshirt Nazi street army.

This post later passed to Ernst Roehm, who eventually
fell afoul of Hitler. In 1934, Hitler decided that to consolidate his power, Roehm and his most important lieuten-
ants had to be killed. The result was a nationwide sweep
dubbed the Blood Purge. Besides Roehm, thousands of

Hitler opponents (real, potential and imagined) were murdered. The initial order for the blood bath was Hitler's, but it was Goering who drew up most of the death lists and oversaw the operation.

Goering was versatile. When circumstances demanded, he could be gracious. The Nazis had built popular support for themselves in part by attacking capitalism. It was Goering's role to assure the wealthy this was mere talk, not to be taken seriously. He helped convince many industrialists to support the Nazis on the grounds that Hitler would restore Germany to a place of honor by rebuilding her military forces. There would be contracts.

Working by friendly solicitation and, after the Nazis got into power, by threat (particularly against Jews), he funneled huge amounts of money to Hitler and had considerable control over the distribution of funds to various Party operations.

He also kept a great deal for himself, spending it on almost every conceivable indulgence. He ate enormously, sometimes eating ten lobsters at a single sitting.

He collected Old Master paintings, medieval tapestries, and an immense trove of jewelry. Much of what he acquired, he simply seized; when he did buy, it was usually at absurdly low prices.

He owned a palace in Berlin and an estate in the country. He was also a morphine addict.

Famous for his gaudy uniforms and flamboyant costumes, he often welcomed guests to his country home dressed as a medieval squire, carrying a boar spear.

Very likely, he knew his oafishness was comforting, particularly to foreign visitors, who saw him as corrupt and ridiculous but understandable. Hitler's act, by contrast, was messianic and mysterious. Goering made the Nazis look manageable.

He played with lion cubs, had a fleet of model boats and an elaborate set of toy trains which he demonstrated with great pride. When the French Ambassador visited, Goering's young nephews, who were also present, called for Uncle Hermann to bring out the French train.

The Ambassador watched as the train duly emerged from its shed and made its way along the labyrinthian trackage. Then a tiny airplane appeared, riding an overhead wire. As the plane passed over the train, it released small wooden bombs, loaded with caps which detonated with scale-model but nevertheless disconcerting explosions.

When it came to the conduct of real events, Goering tried to convince Hitler that attacking Poland was likely to provoke a general European war. He opposed this only because he feared the consequences for Germany, not because of any humanitarian inclinations. He had none.

Among his many services to Hitler was running the terrifying organization which later passed under Heinrich Himmler's control—the Secret State Police, more commonly called the Gestapo (see chapter 35, "Heinrich Himmler"). Together with Himmler, Goering also oversaw the creation of the concentration camps; later, he was among the first to translate "the Fuehrer's wishes on the Jewish question" into the systematic machinery of the Final Solution, which murdered six million Jews.

Goering reached the high point in his career just as the Second World War began, when he was designated as Hitler's successor. His downward slide began not long after, with the failure of the *Luftwaffe* to destroy the Royal Air Force in the Battle of Britain. When that struggle began, Goering had said that if a single enemy bomb fell on Berlin, "You can call me Meier!" (The joke, of course, was that "Meier" is a Jewish name.) When bombs did begin falling on them, Germans took to greeting Goering—when he dared appear in public—as Herr Meier. Sometimes Goering took this jovially, and sometimes not.

The *Luftwaffe*'s failure—and the RAF's magnificent victory—meant Hitler would not be able to invade Britain. Later, Goering promised Hitler the *Luftwaffe* would be able to adequately supply the German forces invading Russia. The complete failure of this operation helped doom Hitler's empire altogether.

Not surprisingly, Goering fell out of favor with Hitler; at about the same time, his drug abuse became more flagrant. In May 1943, while addressing leaders of the German steel industry, his speech slowed and his expression became increasingly vacant. Then he lay his head on the table and went to sleep.

He began painting his fingernails and putting rouge on his cheeks. During meetings, he dipped a hand into a bowl of loose gems he kept by his side and ran the stones playfully through his fingers. His costumes became more outlandish. Hitler, almost never at a loss for words, was struck speechless one day by the sight of Goering in a silken Maharaja's outfit, complete with turban.

The most remarkable uniform Goering ever wore, however, was not distinguished by its flamboyance. The date was April 20, 1945, Hitler's 56th and last birthday. The Russians were closing in on Berlin from the East, British and American forces from the West. Goering turned up for the occasion in a uniform of a color he had never worn before—olive drab, the very color of an American uniform. Hitler took no notice.

That night, Goering, as did many of the inner circle, left Berlin and headed south to the mountains, away from the main thrust of the Russian advance. Hitler and a small entourage remained in the Berlin bunker, grasping at straws and hoping something would stave off the inevitable.

Jockeying for power among Hitler's underlings had been incessant throughout his rule and even now, when the complete pointlessness of this should have been evident, the in-fighting continued. At this moment, Goering made a crucial mistake, sending Hitler a telegram confirming that if Hitler became unable to continue leading the fight he would carry on. Martin Bormann, a top Hitler aide and a skillful intriguer, used this telegram to suggest to Hitler that Goering was planning an overthrow.

Whether Hitler really believed this (it was untrue) or had just decided the time had come to punish Goering for his past failures, he ordered him stripped of all his offices and arrested. It is ironic, but Goering's capture two weeks later by American troops probably saved his life, though only for the time being.

His captors got him off drugs and on a diet; he was soon restored to his early vigor and arrogance. Contemptuous of the International Tribunal convened at Nuremberg to try him and other Nazi leaders, he said he wished he could condense his defense to just three words, "Lick my ass." As it happened, during the trial he apologized for nothing but denied much.

Sentenced to death by hanging, he escaped this fate in much the same way as Hitler had. Two hours before the scheduled execution, he committed suicide with cyanide which had somehow been smuggled into him.

Although all human motive is complex, Goering seems to typify the Hitler follower whose principal drive was for loot. He probably could have found a comfortable place for himself in any large scale criminal operation.

THIRTY-FOUR

Joseph Goebbels

Adolf Hitler, I love you because you are both great and simple. These are the characteristics of the genius.

—GOEBBELS'S DIARY,
APRIL 20, 1926

Joseph Goebbels was the small, sharp-faced one with a limp, the Minister for Propaganda and Enlightenment.

A failed novelist and playwright, acerbic and bitter even as a young man, Goebbels found a suitable outlet for his bile in the Nazi Party's struggle for power in the early 1920s. Although he later became devoted to Hitler, this was not always so.

He fell in at first with Gregor Strasser, a Nazi who opposed Hitler for not being radical enough in his plans for social and economic revolution. Goebbels, with a passionate desire to demolish the old order, saw Nazis and Communists as natural allies, whereas Hitler sought the support of aristocrats and established wealth. As it happens, Goebbels did not say, as a common legend reports, "I demand that the petty bourgeois Adolf Hitler be expelled from the Nazi Party," but he might as well have.

Despite his opposition, Hitler recognized Goebbels's value—his fanaticism, an energetic organizing ability and oratorical skills that rivaled his own. He decided to make Goebbels his man. Always shrewd in assessing just what it was someone else wanted, Hitler offered affection to the angry young radical, and succeeded completely.

Goebbels was proud of the power of his intellect, but in fact his ideas followed his feelings, a process illustrated by diary entries made at the end of July 1926 during a three day visit with Hitler at Berchtesgaden: "He spoils me like a child! The kindly friend and master! . . . To him I feel deeply linked. Now the last of my doubts have vanished. Germany will live! Heil Hitler!"

Goebbels became intensely jealous of other Hitler associates, including Ernst Hanfstaengl, whose duties included entertaining Hitler by playing the piano. When Hitler and Hanfstaengl came to call at the Goebbels home, Goebbels headed off the piano playing by having all the radios in the house turned up full blast.

In time, he hit upon an even better stratagem, playing phonograph records Hitler found more absorbing than music. They were recordings of the Fuehrer's own speeches. Entranced with himself, Hitler would sit listening for hours, all interest in Hanfstaengl and the piano gone.

Goebbels was an unabashed sycophant. One evening after he, Hitler and others of the entourage had seen a film about Frederick the Great, Goebbels pronounced the film magnificent. Then Hitler entered the room and complained that the film had been "a horror—absolute rubbish." Instantly, without any sign of shame or embarrassment, Goebbels rushed to exclaim, "Yes, my Fuehrer. It was feeble, very feeble."

Goebbels was effective at his work, which included staging "spontaneous" demonstrations, as well as helping to design the spectacular Nazi torchlight parades and rallies. Once the Nazis got into power, he took control of all German press, radio and films and utilized them fully for the promulgation of Nazi propaganda, including the "Fuehrer myth."

The substance of the Fuehrer myth was that the leader—Hitler—stood apart from ordinary men. He lived an austere life, sacrificed all for his people, was incorruptible and infallible. If anything went wrong, it was because of his all too human underlings. The Fuehrer myth insured that Hitler remained unsullied, uncriticized, and perfectly free to undertake whatever course of action he chose.

Although he certainly helped promote it, Goebbels gave himself too much credit when he claimed, as he did in conversations with his staff, that he had created the Fuehrer's image. In fact, Hitler had always believed he was a man apart from other men, endowed with extraordinary genius and an historic destiny. The Fuehrer created the Fuehrer myth.

Goebbels's service to Hitler was by no means limited to propaganda. He held the important post of District Leader for Berlin and played a critical role in the Nazi Party's climb to power. He used the Storm Troopers at his disposal for beatings and murder, and he exulted in the violence.

Perhaps the single most significant action Goebbels ever undertook was in the immediate aftermath of the attempt by a group of German Army officers to assassinate Hitler on July 20, 1944. That attempt, made at Hitler's military headquarters in East Prussia, was supposed to precipitate a general overthrow of the Nazi government.

Hitler survived but it was Goebbels, in Berlin, who broke the coup's momentum by asserting the Fuehrer's authority in the capital. Assembling troops to back him up, he converted his mansion into an impromptu combination headquarters, court and prison and soon had many key conspirators under arrest.

Without his quick action, Hitler's career likely would have been terminated on that day, eight months before its actual end. And that would almost certainly have meant an early end to both the war and the Holocaust.

Throughout the entire course of their association, Goebbels continued to disagree with Hitler on one point, persisting in his belief that Nazis and Communists were natural allies. Even after the invasion of Russia, Goebbels advocated breaking off the fight so that Germany and Russia could join together to destroy the "old order" of the West.

On another subject, though, Goebbels was always in agreement with his Fuehrer. He was a Jew-baiter of long standing. Among his more vicious accomplishments was igniting the nationwide anti-Jewish pogrom of November 10, 1938, commonly called "Crystal Night."

As for his private life—Goebbels was married and had six children, but he was almost compulsively adulterous, often with actresses from the movie industry, which he controlled. Hitler joked about Goebbels's affairs and called him his "Minister of the Abdomen" but when Frau Goebbels threatened divorce over one particular liaison, Hitler demanded Goebbels break it off. Divorce would be unseemly for a high-ranking Nazi. Goebbels obeyed, though later he discreetly resumed the affair.

As the end approached for Nazi Germany, Goebbels sometimes acted as though he believed his own propaganda about "miracle weapons" or a saving alliance with either the Russians or the West.

At other times, he brooded about what would constitute a fitting finale, a heroic end insuring immortal glory for Nazism. On April 17, 1945—two weeks before Hitler's death and his own—he made a bizarre speech in which he seemed to assert that immortality was literally achievable through legend. Lecturing his staff on the need for do-or-die courage, he said that some day a motion picture (in color) would undoubtedly be produced about the period they were living through and asked:

Don't you want to play a part in this film, to be brought back to life in a hundred years' time? Hold out now, so that a hundred years hence the audience does not hoot and whistle when you appear on the screen.

Given his subsequent behavior, it is impossible to imagine what kind of movie Goebbels had in mind. When he moved into Hitler's bunker in the center of besieged Berlin he not only brought his wife, but their six children, ranging in age from four years to thirteen.

There is no question the children could have been sent away to safety.

On April 30, Hitler committed suicide. Goebbels had planned to follow suit immediately but, as he told Hitler's valet, "At the last minute I couldn't do it." Instead, he sent a General under a flag of truce over to the nearby Russian line with the incredible proposition that a peace treaty be negotiated. When the General returned with the Russians' flat rejection of anything but unconditional surrender, Goebbels prepared to die.

Even now, there was a good chance the children could have been saved by escape or surrender. But Goebbels, and his wife, did not want them to live. Frau Goebbels doped them with knockout drops and then killed them with cyanide. Accounts differ as to exactly how this was accomplished and there is some evidence the oldest child, a thirteen-year-old girl, realized what was happening and struggled to save her life. To no avail.

Shortly afterward, the monstrous couple left the bunker and went up into the blasted remains of the Chancellery garden. Again, there are varying accounts of exactly how they died. As in the case of Hitler and his wife, the Russian autopsy ascribes the cause of death as solely by self-administered cyanide. Other accounts include self-inflicted gunshot with a coup de grace administered by an S.S. officer. Unlike Hitler, there was never any question about whether Goebbels had somehow escaped with his life.

It is difficult to imagine a man like Goebbels finding a place for himself in any organization that did not value fanaticism, hate, and lunacy.

THIRTY-FIVE

Heinrich Himmler

I owe all I am to Hitler. How can I betray him?

—HIMMLER

Heinrich Himmler was the one with pince-nez glasses, neatly trimmed moustache and the demeanor of a schoolmaster, whose position as head of the S.S. and the Gestapo made him one of the most hated men in Europe.

An early Party member, Himmler retired briefly from active involvement after marrying in 1927, and tried to earn a living raising chickens. Failing at this, he returned to full-time Party work and at the beginning of 1929 was made head of a new unit—the S.S., which at the time had less than 300 members.

The S.S. was originally subordinate to the S.A., the Storm Troopers, whose principal function was street brawling in support of Hitler's political ambitions. The S.A. was large and powerful, and it was because Hitler was not altogether certain of its loyalty that he created the S.S.

S.S. members, distinguished by black uniforms rather than standard-issue S.A. brown, were to serve as Hitler's personal bodyguard. The S.S. motto was "My Loyalty is my Honor," and Hitler dubbed Himmler "the true Heinrich" in recognition of his faithful devotion.

In fact, Himmler kept a dossier of information which might some day be used against the beloved Fuehrer. One favored line of investigation explored the possibility that one of Hitler's grandfathers was Jewish; another, that he was mentally disturbed as the result of syphilis. (Both were almost certainly untrue.)

Himmler was assiduous in building up the S.S. By the time Hitler became Chancellor in 1933, membership had grown to over 50,000.

By the middle of 1934, Hitler felt he had to curb the brownshirt S.A.; its leadership was making demands which threatened his absolute power. He struck with the Blood Purge, a nationwide sweep in which thousands were arrested and shot, including the head of the S.A. The S.S. did most of the killing; thereafter, although the S.A. organization remained, there was never any question of its resuming its former power. The S.S. was supreme.

Ultimately, the S.S. became a state within the state, with over 250,000 members and resources so vast Hitler said, "One day Himmler will be our biggest industrialist." Most of the workers in S.S. factories and mines were slave laborers, who were usually worked literally to death.

Himmler collaborated with Goering in establishing Dachau, the first of what was to become the horrific network of Nazi prison and death camps. He became head of the Gestapo, the Secret Police, the official organ of state terror.

Himmler's authority was enormous. He had the undisputed power to designate almost anyone an enemy and consign them to torture and death. High Nazi Party rank was no guarantee of immunity, with the result that, as one observer noted in his diary, "Except Hitler, no one is entirely without a secret fear of Himmler."

This master of intrigue and terror rarely lost his temper or, for that matter, gave vent to strong feelings of any kind. He is described by those who met him as cold, passionless. Full of self-concern, however, he was often wracked with agony over how Hitler would judge decisions he had made.

Himmler's private life was not particularly extravagant. He was married and had a mistress, who bore him a child.

Unlike Hitler, he was fascinated by the occult and established an Academy of Ancestral Heritage, which was part museum and part mystic lodge. After the war, Allied investigators discovered a pit of ashes in its basement which contained the skull of an infant.

He also believed in telepathic mind control. In 1938, when the chief of the German Army was accused of homosexuality, Himmler convened twelve top S.S. men in a room adjacent to the one in which the General was being questioned. These twelve were to focus their minds and telepathically force the General to admit his scandalous behavior. The effort failed. (As it happened, the charge was later found to be untrue.)

During the war, the S.S. fielded forty combat divisions. These reported through their own chain of command to Himmler and Hitler, and behaved with a viciousness even regular German Army officers found repulsive.

Of course, the work which guaranteed Himmler his immortal infamy was in carrying out Hitler's Final Solution—the attempt to murder all the Jews in Europe.

The S.S. administered the death camps and rounded up the victims. Whenever Hitler issued orders about the genocide, he did so verbally—not in writing—to Himmler, usually with no witnesses present. It was Himmler's role to break the direct line of evidence that linked Hitler to the Final Solution and at the same time insure that the murder machinery operated with the greatest possible speed and effectiveness.

In 1941, Himmler observed a mass shooting of Jews in Russia and nearly fainted. Then he gave way to a rare show of emotion, screaming at the officers in charge because some of the victims had not died outright. This experience inspired his demand that a better means of killing be found, something more efficient. The result was the development of mass murder by gassing.

Himmler regarded his evil deeds as great and good accomplishments. Speaking to a group of S.S. leaders on October 4, 1943, he said that although most Germans were willing to pay lip service to the idea of getting rid of Jews, few had the stomach to do what was required. This provided the measure of the S.S. man. He said:

> Most of you will know what it means to have seen
> one hundred corpses together, or five hundred, or
> a thousand. To have made one's way through that,
> and—some instances of human weakness aside—
> to have remained a decent person throughout, that

is what has made us hard. This is a page of glory
in our history . . .

Later in the same speech, Himmler described the exterminations as "this heaviest of tasks in love to our
people."

He never regretted his monstrous work, but by March
of 1945 was beginning to make nervous jokes about being branded a war criminal. He was, however, by no
means certain this would be his fate and seriously spec-
ulated that Eisenhower might employ him as Chief of
Police for postwar Europe.

He also began exploring the possibility of a separate
armistice with the Western Allies, so that the Nazis
could concentrate on holding off the Russians. Toward
this end, he opened negotiations with Count Folke Bernadotte, a Swedish Red Cross official.

Bernadotte knew the Allies would accept nothing less
than unconditional surrender, but he persuaded Himmler
that releasing concentration camp prisoners could only
help his case. Ultimately, through the efforts of Bernadotte and others, some were freed.

Himmler knew Hitler would regard his negotiations
as treasonous but gambled on them because he believed
Hitler to be terminally ill.

He was mistaken. Word of the negotiations leaked,
and on the evening of April 28, Hitler, enraged by the
defection of "the true Heinrich," threw him out of the
Nazi Party and ordered him arrested. No one seriously
attempted to carry out this order; Himmler was guarded
by a heavily armed personal escort.

After Hitler's suicide, Himmler quickly discovered the

remaining Nazi high command wanted nothing to do with him. He thereupon attempted to slip into anonymity, disguising himself by shaving his moustache, removing his glasses and putting on an eye patch.

The disguise was effective. Although captured by a British patrol, no one realized just who this prisoner was. It wasn't until late the next day that Himmler, perhaps resenting that he was not getting special attention, put his glasses back on and announced himself.

A search of his clothing found a small brass cylinder similar to a lipstick, but the glass ampule of cyanide it should have contained was missing. A first body search found nothing; a second, conducted by a physician, had a grotesque conclusion.

Looking in Himmler's mouth, the doctor spotted one end of the ampule sticking out from between his lower jaw and his cheek. This represented the last shred of power Himmler had left in the world, the power to decide whether he would live or die.

When the doctor made a sudden reach for the ampule, Himmler reacted by biting down on his finger. The doctor jerked away; then, quite deliberately, Himmler bit again, this time breaking the ampule and releasing the cyanide.

Although he collapsed immediately he was not granted instant death. A bucket of water was standing by for just this eventuality, and the doctor and others in the room now grabbed Himmler and lowered his head into the water, trying to wash the poison out of his mouth. Himmler grunted and groaned in agony. The doctor then attempted artificial respiration, but in short time Himmler was dead.

During his life, Heinrich Himmler had been the personification of evil, the author of more terror, torture and murder than any single book could adequately describe, and in all of this he was nothing more than Hitler's servant.

NOTES AND SOURCES

(The first time a source is noted, bibliographic details are given. Thereafter, it is referred to by only an abbreviation. For a complete list, see the bibliography following this section.)

Chapter 1: Hitler's Mustache

The opening quote and story are from *Unheard Witness*, by Ernst Hanfstaengl (J. B. Lippincott, 1957) pp. 69–70. Hitler's response is as Hanfstaengl gave it to investigators from the United States Office of Strategic Services, *OSS Source Book*, Hanfstaengl Interview, p. 12. Although unpublished, the Source Book is available on microfilm from the National Archives.

Hitler combing his hair was described by Frau Traudl Junge in an interview given to Michael Musmanno. Judge Musmanno, then serving in the U.S. Navy, was among those assigned to investigate the exact circumstances of Hitler's death. (H. R. Trevor-Roper performed a similar task for the British.) Musmanno also served as a judge at some of the Nuremberg War Crimes Trials. Junge's quote appears in *Ten Days to Die*, by Michael A. Musmanno (Doubleday, 1950) p. 84.

The dandruff is mentioned in *I Knew Hitler*, by Kurt Ludecke (Scribner's, 1938) p. 273 and p. 629.

Hitler crossing his eyes is mentioned in *Hitler: The Man and the Military Leader*, by Percy Ernst Schramm (Quadrangle Books, 1971) p. 17. Schramm was a professional historian and a reserve officer when he was assigned to Hitler's headquarters staff in 1943. Schramm also mentions the Fuehrer typewriter and the eyeglasses throughout his account, as do others who served at the various Fuehrer headquarters.

"dull, opaque." *The Life and Death of Adolf Hitler*, by Robert Payne (Praeger, 1973) p. 195. Payne met Hitler in 1937, an encounter he describes in *Eyewitness; A Personal Account of a Tumultuous Decade, 1937–46* (Doubleday, 1972) p. 13. F. W. Winterbotham was similarly unimpressed when he met Hitler, *The Nazi Connection* (Harper & Row, 1978) p. 51.

Hitler having his head measured is described in *This Is the Enemy*, by Frederick Oechsner (Little, Brown, 1942) pp. 113–4. Oechsner was the Central European News Manager for United Press before the war.

Von Gruber's testimony is quoted in *Der Fuehrer*, by Konrad Heiden (Houghton Mifflin, 1944) p. 190. Heiden was a German journalist who specialized in covering Hitler and the Nazis from 1922 until June 1933, when he had to flee the country.

"Hitler had an extreme . . . in that state." Professor Hanskarl von Hasselbach, quoted in *The Secret Diaries of Hitler's Doctor*, by David Irving (Macmillan, 1983) p. 34.

Hitler's statement about war and his age is cited in *The War Path*, by David Irving (Viking, 1978) p. 199. Hitler made a similar remark to Baldur von Schirach on 22 August 1939, cited in *Stern* magazine, September 3, 1967, p. 29.

Chapter 2: Hitler's Dog

The opening quote is from a compendium of his meal-time monologues, *Hitler's Secret Conversations 1941–1944* (Farrar, Straus and Young, 1953) entry for the night of 25–26 January 1942, p. 202.

Blondi given by Bormann, *Adolf Hitler*, by John Toland, (Doubleday, 1976) p. 820. Blondi's abilities are described on pages 836 and 846, drawing from his interview with one of Hitler's secretaries, Traudl Junge, and from her unpublished memoirs.

Hitler's disappointment over Blondi's non-pregnancy and her sleeping in his bedroom are described in *Hitler's Secret Life*, by Glenn B. Infield (Stein & Day, 1979) pp. 243 and 202.

The identification of Tornow and other details about Blondi are from *The Death of Adolf Hitler: Unknown Documents from Soviet Archives*, by Lev Bezymenski (Harcourt, Brace & World, 1968) pp. 42–3.

Blondi's effect on strategic planning is recounted by Infield, p. 51, quoting from his interview with Walther Horer, an aide to General Jodl, Chief of Operations for the Armed Forces High Command.

Hitler fondling the pup, Wolf, appears in *The Psycho-*

pathic God: Adolf Hitler, by Robert G. L. Waiter (Basic Books, 1977) p. 413, citing *Hitler Privat*, Ed. by A. Zoller, the memoirs of one of Hitler's secretaries, who is unnamed but generally thought to be Christa Schroeder.

Blondi's death is described in Bezymenski, pp. 42–3, quoting from a recollection by Otto Guensche, a senior Hitler aide. Bezymenski also supplies the Russian postmortem exam on Blondi's corpse, pp. 89–92.

Chapter 3: *Mein Kampf*, Hitler's Book

The opening quote is from a review Thompson wrote which was included in a "Book of the Month Club" pamphlet promoting the Reynal & Hitchcock edition of *Mein Kampf*, an unabridged version published in 1939.

The story of the conversation that set Hitler writing, *Hitler And I*, by Otto Strasser (Houghton Mifflin, 1940) p. 53.

Sales figures for *Mein Kampf* and Hitler's royalties are documented in "Adolf Hitler: Taxpayer," an article by Oron James Hale, published in *American Historical Review*, July, 1955, pp. 830–842. The law requiring the book be bought by cities and given to newlyweds, *I Paid Hitler*, by Fritz Thyssen (Farrar & Rinehart, 1941) p. 173.

The dinner bet is from Strasser, pp. 57–8.

"The White House . . . a different story." *Hitler's Mein Kampf in Britain and America: A Publishing History*, by James J. Barnes and Patricia P. Barnes (Cambridge University Press, 1980) p. 49; for a detailing of

British knowledge, pp. 21–50; for more on the Cranston pamphlet, pp. 19–20.

Chapter 4: Hitler's Names and Titles

The opening quote is from *Young Hitler: The Story of Our Friendship*, by August Kubizek (Allan Wingate, 1954) p. 40.

"Journalists in Austria . . ." *The Rise and Fall of the Third Reich*, by William Shirer (Simon and Schuster, 1960) p. 8.

For more on the complex story of how Alois Schicklgruber became Alois Hitler, see *Adolf Hitler: His Family, Childhood and Youth*, by Bradley F. Smith (Hoover Institution Press, 1967) pp. 29–31.

For a detailed examination and discrediting of the Jewish grandfather story, see *Hitler: Legend, Myth & Reality*, by Werner Maser (Harper & Row, 1973) pp. 9–14.

". . . to prove he was 'uncontaminated' . . ." Heiden, p. 39.

"Hitler liked to point out . . ." Infield, p. 57.

"Herr Wolf . . ." and "Conductor Wolf," *The Mind of Adolf Hitler: The Secret Wartime Report*, by Walter C. Langer (Basic Books, 1972) p. 83 and p. 87. "My little wolfie," Strasser p. 70. "Who's Afraid Of the Big Bad Wolf?" Musmanno, p. 149.

"Ade," Heiden, p. 370. "Adi," "du," Strasser, p. 75 and p. 128. "Ahi," *The Voice of Destruction*, by Hermann Rauschning (G. P. Putnam's Sons, 1940) p. 286.

"Manitou," Heiden, p. 305.

"Der Chef." This is a common usage in the memoirs

and interrogations. See, for example, *Inside the Third Reich*, by Albert Speer (Macmillan, 1970) p. 100.

"...Party members were officially directed..." Strasser, p. 128.

"Anyone at all can be made a president...nobody." *Secret Conversations*, 3–4 Jan 1942, p. 143.

"Grofaz," *Hitler*, by Joachim C. Fest (Harcourt Brace Jovanovich, 1973) p. 633.

"An English journalist noted..." and "If I were the Fuehrer," *Goebbels: The Man Next to Hitler*, by Rudolf Semmler (Westhouse, 1947) p. 96.

Chapter 5: The Nazi Swastika

The opening quote is from Rauschning, p. 223.

"...rah, rah, rah...Sieg Heil!" Hanfstaengl, p. 53.

"Heil Hitler!" *Ibid.*, p. 137. Also, see Ludecke, p. 409.

"Hitler bragged..." *OSS*, p. 922.

"...spring support..." Winterbotham, p. 72.

"...American tourists were warned..." *The Nightmare Years*, by William Shirer (Little, Brown, 1985) p. 117.

"...Social Revolutionary Party..." *A History of National Socialism*, by Konrad Heiden (Alfred A. Knopf, 1940) p. 14. Heiden is sometimes given credit for having coined the word "Nazi." According to this story, National Socialists originally called themselves "Nasos." "Nazi" was supposed to be a slang term meaning bumpkin, and it was Heiden who first used Nazi for Naso. There is only one source for this story, an article in *The Book of the Month Club News*, January 1944, p. 4, and it is qualified with the phrase "...it seems to have been . . .". Heiden himself does not give this account in his books nor is it mentioned in a "Talk of the Town" interview, published in *The New Yorker*, January 1, 1944, pp. 16–7. Perhaps the tale originated from the fact that a Bavarian slang term for bumpkin or scoundrel is "bazi." Thanks to Dr. Joachim Remak for his assistance on this.

". . . Nazi had a 'bad sound' in America . . ." *Berlin Diary*, by William L. Shirer (Alfred A. Knopf, 1941) pp. 494–5.

"Hitler himself rarely referred . . ." Heiden, p. 638.

". . . outlawed its use." Maser, *fn.* p. 257.

Maser describes the Lambach swastika, p. 25.

"Adolf said at that time . . . concept of Germandom." Waite, p. 40, quoting from his interview with Kubizek.

". . . featuring a Swastika flag." This cover sketch is reprinted in *Hitler's Letters and Notes*, by Werner Maser (William Heinemann, 1974) p. 280.

". . . was used by many of the radical nationalist . . ." Heiden, p. 142–3. Also, see *Hitler: A Study in Tyranny*, Completely Revised Edition, by Alan Bullock (Harper & Row, 1962) p. 66.

". . . the color that captured people's attention . . ." Hanfstaengl, p. 152.

Chapter 6: Henry Ford's Nazi Medal

The opening quote is from Ludecke, p. 192.

Ford is described as the first American to receive the medal in the *New York Times*, August 1, 1938, p. 5.

"In 1922, a reporter visiting . . ." *The New York Times*, December 20, 1922, p. 2.

The history of the Dearborn *Independent* is described in *Henry Ford: The Wayward Capitalist*, by Carol Gelderman (The Dial Press, 1981) pp. 219–220.

". . . copies prominently displayed . . ." *The New York Times*, Dec. 20, 1922, p. 2.

". . . Ford's book translated . . ." Gelderman, p. 224.

"Mr. Ford's organization . . . to our Party." *Diplomat Among Warriors*, by Robert Murphy (Doubleday, 1964) p. 23.

". . . a truck and automobile assembly plant in Berlin, Ford agreed . . ." Gelderman, p. 239.

". . . another famous American . . ." *Charles A. Lindbergh and the Battle Against American Intervention in World War II*, by Wayne S. Cole (Harcourt Brace Jovanovich) pp. 41–2.

". . . grave doubts . . ." *Ibid.*, p. 35. Cole goes into this point in detail, quoting the following as characteristic of Lindbergh's views: "Are we deluding ourselves when we attempt to run our governments by counting the number of heads, without a thought of what lies within them?"

". . . will be a lot cheaper . . ." *Secret Conversations*, 15 May 42, p. 324.

Chapter 7: The Fuehrer's Volkswagen

The opening quote is from *Secret Conversations*, 22 June 42, p. 428.

". . . biggest selling car . . ." *Los Angeles Times*, August 13, 1985, I, p. 2.

". . . claiming he dared not drive because if there were . . ." Ludecke, p. 513.

"... he sometimes failed to show up ..." Hanfstaengl, pp. 45–6.

"... bragging about his latest 200 h.p ..." *Hitler— Memoirs of a Confident*, Ed. by Henry Ashby Turner, Jr. (Yale University Press, 1985) pp. 182–3. These are the annotated and edited memoirs of Otto Wagener, a close Hitler associate from 1929 until a fall from grace in the middle of 1933.

"... Baby Hitlers" *The New York Times*, July 3, 1938, X, p. 6.

For a discussion of the respective contributions of Porsche and Hitler, see *Small Wonder: The Amazing Story of the Volkswagen*, by Walter Henry Nelson (Little, Brown and Co., 1965) pp. 42–3.

"... look like a beetle." *The VW Beetle*, by Jonathan Wood (London: Motor Racing Publications, 1979) p. 19.

"... Hitler ordered the building of a ship ..." *Secret Conversations*, 22 June 42, p. 428.

The alternative reading of KdF is cited in *The Twelve Year Reich: A Social History of Nazi Germany 1933– 1945*, by Richard Grunberger (Holt, Rinehart and Winston, 1971) p. 335.

"Hitler gave up ..." *E.g.,* in *Secret Conversations*, 22 June 42, p. 428.

"... the car be called 'Christ' ..." Nelson, p. 58.

For details of the stamp payment plan, *Ibid.,* pp. 63– 68.

"... barely exceeded two hundred ..." *Ibid.,* p. 86.

"His was kept at his mountain estate ..." Infield, p. 188.

The joke about the VW worker appears in Grunberger, p. 29.

"... airplane parts..." and "sixty V-1 'buzz bombs' ..." Nelson, pp. 87–8.

"By the summer of 1945..." "The Volkswagen Story," article in the magazine *After the Battle*, No. 12, 1976, p. 12.

"... more than twenty million..." *Los Angeles Times*, August 13, 1985, I, p. 2.

Chapter 8: Backstage Hitler

The opening quote is from *Hitler and the Final Solution*, by Gerald Fleming (Hamish Hamilton, 1985) p. 18.

"... had himself photographed ..." Fest, p. 518.

The wax head incident is reported by Oechsner, pp. 100–1.

The Hess-Hitler rehearsal, Heiden, pp. 359–60.

Hitler sucking his fingers and chewing his nails, Hanfstaengl, pp. 250, 261, 282; Waite, p. 9, citing Nazi Youth Leader von Schirach.

"teppichfresser," Shirer, *Diary*, p. 137. The question of whether or not Hitler chewed carpets was actually taken up in a memo prepared by the Dutch Legation in Berlin for the Foreign Office. It was reported that he did not. *OSS*, p. 655.

Descriptions of Hitler's rages, their causes and their effects, are abundant. In particular, illustrating the points made here, see Speer, p. 97; Strasser, p. 67; Rauschning, pp. 74, 89.

"... between ten and twelve of these..." Hanfstaengl, pp. 72–3.

"A typical effort began with..." Maser prints the

complete notes for one speech as Appendix B, pp. 335–9.

Hitler's method of dictation is described by Musmanno, pp. 85, 175; and by Maser, pp. 192–3.

For more on Hanussen (Steinschneider), *Gods & Beasts: The Nazis and the Occult*, by Dusty Sklar (Thomas Y. Crowell Co., 1977) pp. 119–22.

". . . a steady stream of reports by telephone." Hanfstaengl, p. 73.

"Kola Dallmann," Maser, p. 230; Wagener, p. 179.

Chapter 9: Hitler Speaks

The opening quote is from Shirer, *Nightmare*, p. 222.

". . . rattle windows in their frames." Hanfstaengl, p. 261.

The dinner table episode is as reported in *Hitler, a Biography*, by Konrad Heiden (Constable, 1936) pp. 102–3.

The cooing voice and its effect are described by Payne, p. 345.

Hanfstaengl notes Hitler's vocal repertoire, p. 126.

Hitler's voice and the effects the World War I gassing had on it are described by Heiden, pp. 187–8; Ludecke, p. 13.

". . . talking to trees." *Hitler's Youth*, by Franz Jetzinger (Hutchinson, 1958) pp. 68–9.

The difficulty of summarizing a Hitler speech was noted by professionals; Schramm (a historian), pp. 71–2; Oechsner (a reporter) p. 64.

"Catcalls and cries of Pfui . . ." quoted by Clinton Beach Conger in his essay in Oechsner, p. 260.

"... a little man stiffened ..." cited by Waite, p. 208.

"Aren't you as enthralled ... with you?" reported by the historian Ena G. Reichmann, who witnessed the remark, cited by Waite, p. 54.

"proclaiming the most secret desires ... whole nation." Strasser, p. 62.

Chapter 10: Hitler in Combat

The opening quote is from a letter Hitler wrote on February 5, 1915, reproduced and translated in Maser, *Letters*, pp. 68–9.

Hitler's draft-dodging and consequent transience are described in a number of biographies, including Maser, *Letters*, pages 28–32. A short book by Bridget Hitler, the wife of Hitler's half brother, purports to describe the months Adolf spent in England but it has been discredited. Hitler's whereabouts during this time are almost completely accounted for. Also, although Hitler reminisced ceaselessly, he never said anything about having been in England.

"... with the delight that a woman ..." Toland, p. 62, quoting from the memoirs of Hans Mend, who served with Hitler.

"We all cursed him ..." Heiden, p. 84.

Hitler's adopting of the Army's command structure is discussed by Bullock, p. 403.

"... audience of clay figures ..." Maser, p. 86.

Hitler's story about the shell burst incident, *I Know These Dictators*, by G. Ward Price (Henry Holt, 1938) p. 40. This is a curious book in that it was written by an English newspaperman who was sympathetic, even at this late date, to Hitler and Mussolini.

The motive for the cover-up about Hitler's Iron Cross, First Class, is described and documented in Maser, p. 88.

Chapter 11: Hitler's Women

The opening quote is from *The Fateful Years*, by Andre Francois-Poncet (Victor Gollancz, 1949) pp. xii–xiii.

"very ladylike . . . dainty little steps." Shirer, *Diary*, p. 137.

"Fraulein Hess" Strasser, p. 36; "Fraulein Anna," Langer, p. 91.

". . . mein Rudi . . . Hesserl." Hanfstaengl, p. 129.

"No one with family . . . street fighting." *Ibid.*, p. 82.

For more on the persecution of homosexuals, see *The Nazi Extermination of Homosexuals*, by Frank Rector (Stein & Day, 1981).

Langer describes Hitler's perversion on p. 134. Also, see Langer, pp. 167–8 and 170. Utilizing information which became available after the war, Robert G. L. Waite was able to further substantiate the diagnosis and study its implications. See Waite's *The Psychopathic God* (Basic Books, 1977).

For more on Stefanie, see Kubizek, pp. 38–49.

". . . detailed medical evidence . . ." *E.g.*, a medical report dated January 10, 1940 describes a negative result for a Wassermann and other V.D. tests. Irving, *Secret Diaries*, p. 288. Also, see the interview with one of Hitler's doctors, Ernst Schenck in *American Medical News*, Oct. 11, 1985, p. 39.

". . . varicose vein squad . . ." Rauschning, p. 259.

"little Wolfie," Strasser, p. 70.

The pornographic books in Hitler's library are described by Hanfstaengl, pp. 49–50; the films, Waite, p. 233, citing an interview with Hanfstaengl; also *OSS*, p. 628.

For Maria Reiter, see Waite, pp. 223–5.

For Henny Hoffmann and her father, see Strasser, pp. 70–1; *OSS*, p. 918; Langer, p. 88–9.

For Jenny Haug, see Hanfstaengl, p. 54.

Geli Raubal's place in Hitler's life is described in most of the memoirs of people who knew him at this time. Strasser, pgs. 203–4, speculates that Hitler had Geli murdered, but most historians conclude that she did, indeed, shoot herself.

"Now I am altogether free . . . for this." Turner, p. 222.

Hitler's interest in music hall performances, *OSS*, pp. 227 and 746; Speer, p. 130.

Mueller told her story to A. Zeissler, a motion picture director, who was interviewed for the *OSS* report, pp. 921–2; Langer, p. 171.

Eva and Hitler's bedroom arrangement is described in "The Hitler I Knew," by Heinz Linge, published in the Chicago *Daily News*, Oct. 28, 1955, p. 15. Linge was Hitler's valet.

"I have nothing . . . as a man." Hanfstaengl, pp. 289–90.

"I have overcome the need . . ." Turner, p. 222.

Klara's portrait over Hitler's bed and his practice of carrying her picture, Waite, p. 141, citing a number of sources.

Chapter 12: William Patrick Hitler

The opening quote is from an article William Patrick wrote for *Paris-Soir*, August 5, 1939, quoted by Maser, pp. 5–6.

The relationship between Paula and Adolf is described in William Patrick's *OSS* interview, p. 929.

Paula's interventions are described in Maser, p. 26 and p. 354 *fn*. 17.

"I cannot . . . war." *Twenty Letters to a Friend*, by Svetlana Alliluyeva (London: Hutchinson & Co., 1967) p. 173. Svetlana is Stalin's daughter.

Alois's first Berlin cafe and the "A. Hitler" menu cards are described by Oechsner, pp. 89–90. The opening of the subsequent "Tea Room Alois" is described in the *New York Times* (September 17, 1937) p. 4. For his capture and release by the British, *ibid*., August 4, 1945, p. 2.

The principal source for the account of William Patrick's association with Adolf is the interview he himself gave an *OSS* interrogator, *OSS*, pp. 924–30. Also, "Hitler vs Hitler", *Time Magazine* (April 10, 1939) p. 20.

William naming his son "Adolf," Toland, p. 383, *fn*.

Maser's announcement was reported by *The Sunday Times* (London) October 30, 1977, p. 1. and *Time Magazine* (November 14, 1977) p. 45.

"How very much . . . Germany!" Turner, p. 33.

Among sources describing the kidnapping, breeding and extermination of children are *The Nazi Doctors*, by Robert Jay Lifton (Basic Books, 1986) p. 43; Grunberger, pp. 246, 280; Toland, p. 868, *fn*. For an interview with a man born in one of the breeding camps, see *San*

Francisco Chronicle (November 24, 1985) "Punch Section", p. 3 *et fol.*

"For my part . . . belong to me." *Secret Conversations*, entry for night of 27–28 July 1941, p. 14.

". . . a sacrifice of eight to ninety . . ." Heiden, p. 323.

Chapter 13: Hitler the Hypochondriac

The opening quote is cited by Toland, p. 268.

". . . including one which contained poisonous wood alcohol." *OSS*, p. 936.

Dr. Ernst Schenck affirms that it was Hitler's idea, not Morell's, that he keep taking "Dr. Koester's," on page 40 of his interview in *American Medical News*, Oct. 11, 1985. Hitler overdosing on 18 of the pills is described in Musmanno, p. 50.

". . . a leg rash so severe he had to give up wearing boots." Irving, *Diaries*, p. 23. Also, Maser, p. 212.

". . . a bit of a screwball." Speer, p. 105.

"Sometimes the capsules dissolved . . ." Irving, *Diaries*, p. 96. "Human feces . . .", Speer, *Playboy* magazine, July 1971, p. 190.

". . . 'fresh air poisoning'." O'Donnell, p. 36.

"He was sure his gut would feel better . . ." Schenck, p. 39.

". . . including amphetamines . . ." and ". . . total of ninety-two different . . ." *Ibid.*, p. 39.

". . . leeches . . ." Irving, *Diaries*, pp. 87–88.

". . . insisting on administering them himself." *Ibid.*, p. 34.

"Largely because of the tremors . . ." See the Schenck

article. Also, Maser, pp. 209–233, particularly p. 231 and Irving, *Diaries*, p. 169.

"Himmler suspected . . . syphilis . . ." Maser, 195–6. For the negative Wassermann, see Irving, *Diaries*, p. 288.

Chapter 14: Hitler's Diet

The opening quote is from *OSS*, p. 575.

". . . gnawing chunks of sausage . . ." Ludecke, p. 96.

"It is like eating a corpse!" *The Psychology of Dictatorship*, by G. M. Gilbert (Ronald Press, 1950) p. 62. Gilbert was assigned to study the mental condition of the defendants at the Nuremberg War Crimes trials. Goering reported this remark to him.

Many contemporaries noticed a connection with Geli's death but it is Wagener who reports the autopsy in particular, pp. 221–2.

". . . corpse tea . . ." Speer, p. 301.

". . . a pudding made from his own blood." Schenck, p. 41.

Hitler's foods are drawn from a number of sources including Schenck, p. 41, Hanfstaengl, p. 228, Musmanno, p. 149.

The story of Fraulein Kunde is told in Musmanno, pp. 82–83.

"Imagine me going around with a potbelly!" Speer, p. 301.

Hitler's devotion to chocolate and the seven teaspoons of sugar are from *OSS*, p. 935.

". . . iceberg of whipped cream." *The Inner Circle:*

Memoirs, by Ivone Kirkpatrick (Macmillan, 1959) pp. 96–7.

"... adding sugar to a glass of wine." Hanfstaengl, p. 41.

Hitler's drinking habits are described in a number of sources, including Musmanno, p. 149, Hanfstaengl, p. 41. For more on the specially brewed beer, see Waite, p. 26.

Hitler's claim he gave up drinking out of respect for the poor is reported by Wagener, p. 34. For the story about the certificate, *Secret Conversations*, night of 8–9 Jan 42, p. 160.

"... Hitler's favorite drink was tea ..." Linge, October 26. Hitler's remark about coffee appears in Wagener, p. 67.

"... food tasters sample every dish." *Hitler's Personal Security*, by Peter Hoffmann (Macmillan, 1979) pp. 153 and 155.

Hanfstaengl describes Hitler's early poison phobia on p. 69.

"the fluid ... my veins." Musmanno, p. 50.

Hitler's order removing cigarettes from the Christmas packages, Infield, pp. 190–191.

Hitler's hope of manufacturing cigarettes without nicotine, Irving, *The War Path*, p. 106.

The open smoking is mentioned in almost all memoirs and interviews of people who were there, including Musmanno, p. 205, who also mentions Hitler eating meat.

Chapter 15: I Was Hitler's Dentist

The opening quote is from the article, "Dental Evidence in the Postmortem Identification of Adolf Hitler, Eva Braun, and Martin Bormann" by Reidar F. Sognnaes, in *Legal Medicine Annual, 1976* (Prentice-Hall) p. 225.

". . . still as a lamb . . ." Musmanno, p. 202. Linge's version is reported by Bezymenski, p. 10.

". . . Hitler maintained his composure . . ." Schramm, p. 18, *fn.*

For detailed data on the condition of Hitler's teeth, see Sognnaes, pp. 179–81. Also, Schenck, p. 36.

". . . first resort was always drugs. . . ." Blaschke, quoted from an unpublished Musmanno interview by Infield, p. 182.

The Blaschke entry in the yearbook is reproduced by Sognnaes, p. 223; biographical details, pp. 223–25.

". . . I would never have been Hitler's dentist." Musmanno, pp. 88–9.

For the circumstances of Blaschke's interrogation, Sognnaes, pp. 173 and 196. Also, Schramm, p. 18, *fn.*

Chapter 16: Hitler's Wardrobe

The opening quote is from *Secret Conversations*, 17 Feb 42, p. 258, as is his suggestion to Himmler. Six months later, he was still complaining about having had to give up *lederhosen*, and still planning to have "an SS Highland Brigade in leather shorts." 12 Aug 42, p. 511.

". . . an extra pocket . . . for the pistol." A number of sources mention this, including Ludecke, p. 97.

Hitler carefully hanging up his belt and holster is de-

scribed by Fest, pp. 134–5, citing a German historian
who knew Hitler and witnessed this, Karl Alexander von
Muller.

"... clothes were padded ..." *E.g.* Oechsner, p. 91.

"... bulletproof vest." *E.g.* Payne, p. 291.

"... heavy as a cannonball ..." quoted in Hoffmann,
p. 153.

"... common man appeal ..." An observation made
by Janet Flanner, *Janet Flanner's World* (Harcourt
Brace Jovanovich, 1979) p. 8.

"... if Hitler's utterly mediocre ... greatest assets."
Ludecke, p. 185.

"... specially burnished to a higher sheen ..." *The
Nazi Olympics*, by Richard D. Mandell (Macmillan,
1971) p. 105.

"... pre-tied ties." Waite, citing Hitler's valet, p. 19.

"... a calf-length nightshirt ..." *OSS*, p. 923.

The birthday pajamas are described by Oechsner,
p. 109.

"... full-length white underwear." *The History of the
German Resistance 1993–1945*, by Peter Hoffmann
(MIT Press, 1977) p. 42.

"... the most sacred and dear to me ... survive the
outcome." *My New Order*, a collection of Hitler's
speeches, Edited with Commentary Raoul de Roussy de
Sales (Reynal & Hitchcock, 1941) p. 689.

Chapter 17: Hitler's Bookshelf

The opening quote is from Rauschning, p. 237.

"Colleagues complained ..." *E.g.*, Ludecke, p. 631.

For more on the anti-Semitic pamphlets Hitler read in

Vienna, see *The War Against the Jews 1933–1945*, by Lucy S. Dawidowicz (Bantam Books, 1976) pp. 9–10.

Among those who have shown how completely Hitler adopted Le Bon's ideas are Maser, pp. 260–61 and Waite, p. 122.

"... began a book by looking at its end..." Schramm, p. 73. Wagener notes Hitler scanning quickly through newspapers, looking for only that which will confirm his views, p. 67.

"... 'intrinsic truth'." Rauschning, p. 238.

"One of his secretaries later recalled..." Bullock, p. 398.

"... semi-pornographic..." Hanfstaengl, pp. 49–50.

For the briefing book and the uses to which Hitler put it, Speer, p. 231.

"... Goering curried favor..." Oechsner, p. 97.

"I owe my first... to the world." *Secret Conversations*, 17 Feb 42, p. 257.

Hitler wanting his Generals to study May is cited by Infield, p. 231, quoting from the memoirs of Heinz Linge, Hitler's valet.

Chapter 18: Hitler at the Movies

The opening quote and anecdote are from "I Was Hitler's Buddy," by Reinhold Hanisch, *The New Republic*, April 5, 1939, p. 242.

"... not adept with the projector..." Speer, p. 36. Also, see *OSS*, p. 921.

"... Emil Jannings..." Speer, p. 36; "... Greta Garbo..." Bullock, p. 387; "... Shirley Temple."

Waite, p. 9, citing the unpublished papers of Fritz Wiedemann, one of Hitler's adjutants.

". . . Charlie Chaplin . . ." Speer, p. 36.

Lives of a Bengal Lancer required viewing for the S.S., Kirkpatrick, p. 94.

King Kong, Hanfstaengl, pp. 232–3; Hradcany Castle, Payne, p. 338.

Hitler's calls and visits to the studios, *OSS*, p. 921.

". . . a perverted voyeur." Waite, p. 233, citing conversations with Hanfstaengl.

The Maharaja's film is described by Payne, p. 461, citing an interview with Hans Bauer, Hitler's personal pilot.

Hitler giving up features, then newsreels, Bullock, p. 720; his reaction to the bombing of Warsaw, Speer, p. 227. He made his promise to endure all hardships in his speech of Sept. 1, 1939, *My New Order*, p. 689.

There is no question the executions were filmed for Hitler but his valet and adjutant deny he ever looked at the footage. Speer reports he "loved the film and had it shown over and over again." Interview in *Playboy*, July, 1971, p. 193. Also, a number of sources, including Musmanno, p. 147 and Hoffmann, *Resistance*, p. 528, report that Hitler frequently showed photographs of the executions to members of his entourage.

Chapter 19: Hitler Laughs

The opening quote is from *Hitler's Interpreter*, by Dr. Paul Schmidt (Macmillan, 1951) p. 71.

"The Phipps routine . . . giddy contempt . . ." *OSS*, p. 417.

"... a caricature of Matsuoka ..." Semmler, p. 26.

"... Robert Ley ..." Infield, p. 133; Speer, pp. 143–4.

"... a goebbels and a goering?" *OSS*, pp. 631–2.

"... the butt of a series ... dead microphone ..." Speer, pp. 124–5.

The telephone joke on Ribbentrop, *Ibid*, p. 97.

For a detailed description of the Hanfstaengl joke, see Hanfstaengl, pp. 292–306. At the time he wrote his account, Hanfstaengl was still not sure it had been a joke, but Speer records Hitler's reaction when it backfired, p. 127.

"... serious criminal offense in Nazi Germany ..." For some specific instances, see Flanner, p. 19 and Grunberger, p. 331.

The broken treaties joke, Speer, p. 180.

"Look, I poach . . . not their flashlights." *Hitler's War*, by David Irving (The Viking Press, 1977) p. 289.

Chapter 20: Games the Fuehrer Played

The opening quote is from *The Secret Life of Adolf Hitler*, a book based on a television documentary of the same name, produced for WPIX by William Cooper, Jr. and Walter D. Engels. Text adapted from the script by Eldorous L. Dayton. Published by The Citadel Press, New York, 1960, p. 6.

"... dressing game ..." Waite, p. 9, quoting from the memoirs of Heinz Linge, Hitler's valet.

"... direct eye contact ... against the victor." Speer, p. 100.

"Beaver," Waite. p. 9.

Dr. Ellsberg's essay is titled "The Political Uses of Madness," part of a series, *The Act of Coercion: A Study of Threats in Economic Conflicts and War*, which he delivered as the 1959 Lowell Institute Lectures at the Boston Public Library. "The Political Uses of Madness" is not published and was very kindly supplied by the author.

"I call it the Madman Theory . . . to stop the war." *Without Fear or Favor*, by Harrison E. Salisbury (Times Books, 1980) p. 54.

". . . the planes were being secretly flown . . ." Irving, *Path*, p. 125.

". . . trying to break the bank?" *Ibid.*, p. 256.

". . . dead men had been . . . bullets fired into them." *The Labyrinth*, by Walter Schellenberg (Harper & Bros. 1956) pp. 49–50. Although Schellenberg did not participate in this particular atrocity, he was a high-ranking S.S. officer, eventually a top aide to Himmler.

Chapter 21: Hitler and Music

The opening quote is from Kubizek, p. 140.

". . . didn't care much for Mozart, Beethoven or Bach." Schramm, p. 68.

For the *Rienzi* story, Kubizek, pp. 64–6.

". . . a member of his . . . a Party of his own." Wagener, p. 217.

Hitler ordering the Storm Troopers to corral an audience for *Der Miestersinger*, Speer, pp. 60–1.

"*Aida,*" Irving, p. 230.

"*Les Preludes,*" Speer, p. 130.

"Strauss and Lehar . . ." Schramm, p. 68. "Dorothy,"

"The Metropole," *OSS*, pp. 227, 746. Also, Speer, p. 130.

Kannenberg and "Who's Afraid of the Big Bad Wolf?" Musmanno, p. 149.

"Hitler approved . . . mere 'acrobatics.' Schramm, p. 68.

". . . waltzes . . . a factor in the downfall . . ." Hanfstaengl, p. 135.

". . . picked out tunes . . . flute." Oechsner, p. 88.

". . . it was the composer who had erred." Waite, p. 43, quoting A. Zoller, *Privat*.

Chapter 22: The Art Dictator

The opening quote is cited in *Hitler and the Artists*, by Henry Grosshans (Holmes & Meier, 1983) p. 11.

Hitler's experiences with the Vienna Academy are described in detail by Maser, pp. 39–41.

"His watercolors were good enough . . ." Maser, *Letters & Notes*, p. 34; all standard biographies describe the postcards, and a number of the advertising posters are described by Heiden, p. 54.

The partner was Reinhold Hanisch, "I Was Hitler's Buddy," *The New Republic*, April 5, 1939, in particular, pp. 40–1.

". . . doodles . . ." Hanfstaengl, pp. 142 and 151; for the 1925 sketch, Speer, p. 74.

For Hitler's views on modern art, see his speech on the occasion of the opening of the House of German Art, translated and published in *Theories of Modern Art*, by Herschel B. Chipp (University of California Press, 1968) pp. 474–83.

For Hitler's theories about Jews promoting modern art, *Secret Conversations*, p. 300.

". . . people who bought pictures here could be sure . . ." *Ibid.*, p. 411.

The picture-kicking episode is described by Shirer, *Nightmare Years*, p. 133.

For accounts of the Degenerate Art Exhibit and the burning of the pictures, see Chipp, p. 474, *fn*; also, Grunberger, 423–6.

Chapter 23: Hitler the Builder

The opening quote is from Speer, p. 80.

". . . give shopkeepers . . . to you!" *Secret Conversations*, 19 Oct 41, p. 62.

". . . 'Oriental, Semitic' . . ." Heiden, p. 365.

"Wanting to tear down the Berlin Town Hall . . ." Maser, *Letters & Notes*, p. 134.

". . . grand halls and salons . . . smaller dignitaries." Speer, p. 103.

"When the diplomats . . . shiver and shake." *Ibid.*, pp. 113–4.

". . . worried how his palaces and stadiums would look . . ." *Ibid.*, p. 56; for the final fate of the new Chancellery, p. 116. But Hitler's mind was chewing on this problem well before he met Speer. See Wagener, p. 73 and Heiden, p. 367.

The window fiasco, Speer, pp. 85–6.

Francois-Poncet is quoted in Oechsner, p. 78.

". . . visited it less than half a dozen times." Speer, p. 84; ". . . heart palpitations." Infield, p. 97.

". . . more concrete than was allotted . . ." *The Bunker:*

The History of the Reich Chancellery Group, by James P. O'Donnell (Houghton Mifflin, 1978), quoting an interview with Speer, p. 54.

Chapter 24: Private Finances

The opening quote is from a German tax official's memo, translated and published in Hale, p. 840.

". . . left large tips . . ." Hanfstaengl, pp. 160–1.

The *Mein Kampf* sales figures are given by Hale, p. 839.

". . . also received generous regular payment for the articles he wrote . . ." Heiden, p. 279.

"The Hearst . . . thousands of dollars per article." *German Big Business and the Rise of Hitler*, by Henry Ashby Turner (Oxford University Press, 1985) pp. 154–5.

"Hitler became furious on one occasion . . ." *Secret Conversations*, 6 July 42, p. 458.

For more detail on Hitler's personal income and his tax evading, Turner, pp. 153–4.

"Writer" to "Reich Chancellor" and the amount Hitler was in arrears, Hale, p. 830; for his becoming officially tax-exempt and for the address plate incident, pp. 840–1.

For Hitler's arrangement with Hoffmann, Hanfstaengl, p. 184. It was Hoffmann who happened to take the photograph of Hitler in the crowd in Munich in 1914, when war with Russia was announced (see chapter 10, "Hitler in Combat"). Also, Hitler met Eva Braun (see chapter 11 "Hitler's Women") when she was working as an assistant to Hoffmann.

"He received only . . . stamp's face value." Speer, p. 87.

The most expensive Hitler stamp is listed at $1.00 in standard catalogues. Most go for about twenty cents. One of the Allied servicemen who benefited was Stuart A. Clark, a Canadian Army officer, who was kind enough to describe his adventure in a letter to the author.

". . . from ten percent to fifteen." Hale, p. 837.

"Additionally, a law was passed requiring . . ." *I Paid Hitler*, by Fritz Thyssen (Farrar & Rinehart, Inc. 1941) p. 173.

"Adolf Hitler Endowment Fund of German Industry." Speer, p. 87.

". . . didn't feel as heavy as in previous years." Musmanno, p. 14–5.

". . . not declared legally dead until October, 1956. *New York Times*, Oct. 26, 1956, p. 5:2.

". . . his will declared invalid . . ." *Selling Hitler*, by Robert Harris (Pantheon Books, 1986) p. 53.

Chapter 25: Mussolini, Stalin, France

The opening quote is from Francois-Poncet, p. 239.

"To impress Mussolini . . . got them yet." Heiden, p. 279.

". . . gramophone with just seven records." *Duce!* by Richard Collier (Viking, 1971) p. 118.

Mussolini making Hitler tail after him is described by Oechsner, p. 103; the toy cannon, p. 92.

"Macaroni . . . basta." *Spandau: The Secret Diaries*, by Albert Speer (Macmillan, 1976), pp. 125–6.

"Mussolini Platz," Speer, *Inside the Third Reich*, p. 110.

". . . three or four teeth pulled." Bullock, p. 605.

". . . he would employ Stalin . . ." Speer, *Inside*, p. 306; "In his own way he is a hell of a fellow!" *Secret Conversations*, 22 July 42, p. 476.

". . . alive and living in Spain." *Hitler: The Survival Myth*, by Donald M. McKale (Stein and Day, 1981) p. 72.

". . . keeping their pictures in a place of honor . . ." *Newsweek* Magazine, November 3, 1975, p. 41.

Chapter 26: Hitler and the USA

The opening quote is from Hanfstaengl, p. 234.

The definitive account of the facts behind the Hitler's American land myth is provided by *The Range Ledger of Cheyenne Wells,* Colorado, January 28, 1976.

For more on "Amerika," see *Hoffmann, Personal Security*, pp. 67–8 and 71.

"Ludecke studied the Klan . . . a Nazi auxiliary." Ludecke, pp. 205–8.

"We shall soon . . . in America." Rauschning, p. 70.

". . . defeat of the South . . . a tragedy." *Ibid.*, p. 68.

For more on the lengths Hitler went to maintain neutrality, see *Prelude to Downfall: Hitler and the United States, 1939–1941*, by Saul Friedlander (Alfred A. Knopf, 1967), particularly pp. 49–55.

". . . many feared American entry . . ." Shirer, *Rise and Fall*, p. 894 *fn*.

"I'll never believe . . . like a hero." *Secret Conversations*, entry for 5 Jan 42, p. 149.

". . . skyscrapers were particularly vulnerable . . ."
Ibid., entry for 28 Aug 42, p. 543.

". . . she could go to Hollywood . . ." *The Hitler File:
A Social History of Germany and the Nazis, 1918–1945*,
by Frederic V. Grunfeld (Random House, 1974) p. 276.

Chapter 27: Hitler's Horoscope

The opening quote is given in *Urania's Children*, by
Ellic Howe (William Kimber, 1967) p. 93.

". . . easily flattered . . ." Hanfstaengl, p. 69.

For more on the Hitler-Hanussen association, Sklar,
pp. 199–22; also, Langer, p. 32.

". . . Hitler occasionally joked about the Ebertin . . ."
Howe, pp. 236–7, quoting p. 76 of A. Zoller, *Hitler Privat*.

For more on De Wohl, see Howe, pp. 204–18; also,
Black Boomerang, by Sefton Delmer (Secker & Warburg, 1962) pp. 131–2.

For more on *Aktion Hess*, see Howe, pp. 193–4.

"Oddly enough . . . for their profession!" *The Goebbels Diaries, 1939–41*, Translated & Edited by Fred
Taylor (G. P. Putnam's Sons, 1983) p. 408.

The consulting of horoscopes by Goebbels and Hitler
and the joy at their apparent salvation is described by
Trevor-Roper, pp. 109–13.

Chapter 28: Hitler's Atomic Bomb

The opening quote is from *Alsos*, by Samuel A. Goudsmit (Sigma Books, 1947) p. 83. Dr. Goudsmit led the
Allied team that followed in the wake of Eisenhower's

advance through Europe, trying to determine if Germany was close to building a bomb.

". . . he became immensely excited . . ." Speer, p. 368.

For detailed information and photographs of the damage done by the V-2s, see *After the Battle* Magazine, No. 6, 1974, pp. 32–5.

". . . to assure themselves London was still there." Los Alamos scientist Phillip Morrison described this BBC monitoring in an interview published in the *Los Angeles Times*, August 5, 1985, Part I, p. 1.

For more on Lenard's beliefs and influence, Goudsmit, p. 83; Speer, p. 228.

For more on the efforts of Heisenberg and others to exonerate relativity theory from being "Jewish," see Goudsmit, particularly pp. 113–5 and 151–4.

". . . the world he planned on ruling being turned into a fireball." Speer, p. 226.

The bitter rivalries within the Hitler state are described in most histories and biographies. For a concise overview, see *Hitler's Mistakes*, by Ronald Lewin (William Morrow & Co., 1984), pp. 58–73.

". . . a bomb could not be built . . ." Speer, p. 227; tungsten/uranium, p. 228.

". . . the problem of nuclear . . . next week." Maser, p. 136.

The Gestapo effort is described by Goudsmit, pp. 89–90.

Chapter 29: The Olympic Patron

The opening quote is from Price, p. 193.

". . . an invention . . . National Socialists." *Hitler's*

Games, by Duff Hart-Davis (Harper & Row, 1986) pp. 45–6.

"If Germany is to stand host . . . magnificent." *Ibid.*, p. 47.

". . . particularly in the United States . . . people were demanding . . ." For more on this, see *The Nazi Olympics*, by Richard D. Mandell, (Macmillan, 1971) pp. 69–81.

For a review of the anti-Jewish sports decrees, *Ibid.*, p. 60.

"It is dangerous . . ." and "Death to Jews . . ." *The House That Hitler Built*, by Stephen H. Roberts, (Harper & Bros., 1938) p. 264; also, see Shirer, pp. 233–4.

". . . a small point of Olympic protocol . . ." and "You will . . . be given" Mandell, pp. 93–4.

". . . despite the pleas of associates . . ." Hart-Davis, p. 156.

". . . was a war . . . he scowled." Roberts, p. 18.

"Do you . . . a Negro." Hart-Davis, p. 177.

"..closer to animals than men." Speer, p. 73. "The Americans ought to be ashamed . . . by Negroes." Hart-Davis, p. 177.

". . . for all time . . . the measurements." Speer, p. 70.

Chapter 30: Why Didn't Somebody Kill Him?

The opening quote is from *Ambassador Dodd's Diary*, Ed. by William E. Dodd, Jr. and Martha Dodd (Harcourt, Brace and Co., 1941) pp. 237–8.

"Nearly a dozen attempts . . ." These are reviewed by Peter Hoffmann, *The History of the German Resistance*

1933–1945 (The MIT Press, 1977) pp. 251–3.

". . . saying had they been idealists willing to risk . . ." *Secret Conversations*, 3 May 42, p. 366.

". . . bulletproof limousines as Christmas presents . . ." Semmler, p. 61.

". . . a law forbade throwing a bouquet." Flanner, p. 21.

The Elser attempt and his death are described by Hoffmann, *History*, pp. 256–8. Also, see Schellenberg, pp. 84–6, and 91–2 for a firsthand description of Elser in prison.

For more on the Army plot and Czechoslovakia, Hoffmann, *History*, pp. 95–6. Also, see *The German Generals Talk*, by B. H. Liddell Hart (William Morrow & Co. 1948) pp. 32–3.

For more detail on the Stauffenberg attempt, *Hitler's Personal Security*, by Peter Hoffmann (Macmillan Press, 1979) pp. 245–53. Also, *To Kill the Devil*, by Herbert Molloy Mason, Jr. (Norton, 1978) pp. 166–9. Among other books devoted to this episode is *The Secret War Against Hitler*, by Fabian von Schlabrendorff, (Pittman Publishing, 1965). Schlabrendorff, was one of the few conspirators to survive the war.

". . . would be like anarchy." Hoffmann, *Security*, p. 194. Also, see *The Times*, London, March 16, 1985, p. 6 for an essay examining the subject.

For an account of the raid against the Berghof and surrounding buildings, see *After the Battle* Magazine, No. 9, 1975, p. 20.

"would be followed by the complete extermination of all Jews . . ." Langer, p. 210.

Chapter 31: Was Hitler Really Anti-Semitic?

The opening quote is from *Berlin Alert*, by Truman Smith (Hoover Institution Press, 1984) p. 57.

"It is essential . . . abstract one." Rauschning, p. 237.

". . . Jews as an alien influence." Kubizeck, p. 52. In *Mein Kampf*, Hitler claims he became an anti-Semite only in later years, after serious study. This claim has been thoroughly discredited by his biographers.

For a review of the history of 19th Century anti-Semitism and German identity, see *The War Against the Jews: 1933–1945*, by Lucy S. Dawidowicz (Holt, Rinehart and Winston, 1975) pp. 29–43. Professor Dawidowicz's book is a comprehensive master work on Hitler's attempt to exterminate the Jews in Europe.

Dr. Bloch published his memoirs in *Collier's* magazine, March 15, 1941, p. 9 and March 29, 1941, p. 69.

". . . the Jews were sorry now . . ." Musmanno, p. 100.

Hitler's preference for the Jewish art dealers, and debating Zionism with a Jewish friend, Hanisch, p. 272.

For taking a friend to observe a Jewish wedding, and joining the Anti-Semite Union, Kubizeck, p. 187.

". . . the total removal . . . our midst." Maser, *Letter & Notes*, p. 215.

". . . a Communist . . . a loyal Nazi." *Secret Conversations*, entry for 2 Aug 41, pp. 16–7. Also, Semmler, p. 47.

"Once I am really in power . . . annihilation of the Jews." *Hitler and the Final Solution*, by Gerald Fleming (Hamish Hamilton, 1985) p. 17.

"Conscience is a Jewish . . . like circumcision." Rauschning, p. 223.

". . . laughed in delight when given reports of violence . . ." Bullock, p. 397.

For anti-Jewish legislation, see Dawidowicz, pp. 58–59.

"You must understand . . . what you cannot do." Quoted by Saul Friedlander in his Introduction to Fleming, p. xxx.

Gerald Fleming's *Hitler and the Final Solution* is a comprehensive rebuttal to the extraordinary claim sometimes made that Hitler was unaware of the death camps or knew of them only vaguely.

". . . Hitler raged . . . prisoners left behind . . ." Schellenberg, p. 395.

For full text of the Political Testament, see any standard biography or history, *e.g.*, Shirer, 1123–8.

Chapter 32: Hitler's Corpse

The opening quote is from *Khrushchev Remembers with an Introduction, Commentary and Notes*, by Edward Crankshaw (Little, Brown, 1970) p. 219.

For a survey of Hitler survival stories see *Hitler: the Survival Myth*, by Donald M. McKale (Stein and Day, 1981). Interested readers might also profit from *Imagining Hitler*, by Alvin H. Rosenfeld (Indiana University Press, 1985).

As to how the details of Hitler's death were determined, see *The Last Days of Hitler*, by H. R. Trevor-Roper (Macmillan, 1978). Trevor-Roper conducted the British investigation. For methods of comparing different testimonies to confirm their veracity, see in particular, pp. xxiii–xxiv.

"On July 17th, Stalin . . ." *Speaking Freely*, by James F. Byrnes (Harper and Bros., 1947) p. 68. Secretary of State Byrnes participated in this conversation.

"The book admits . . ." *The Death of Adolf Hitler: Unknown Documents from Soviet Archives*, by Lev Bezymenski (Harcourt, Brace & World, Inc., 1968) p. 66.

". . . 'manly resolve' . . ." *Ibid.*, p. 72.

In *The Psychopathic God*, p. 422, Robert Waite speculates that Eva Braun fired a coup de grace shot into Hitler's head after he bit down on his cyanide capsule, but even this version admits a gunshot, which the Russians dismiss altogether. It is undisputed that Eva committed suicide solely by cyanide.

Dr. Sognnaes details his researches and explains how he arrived at his conclusive identification in "Dental Evidence in the Postmortem Identification of Adolf Hitler, Eva Braun, and Martin Bormann", *Legal Medical Annual*, 1976, (Prentice-Hall, 1977).

". . . final disposition of Hitler's remains . . ." Bezymenski, p. 66.

Chapter 33: Hermann Goering

The opening quote is cited by Musmanno, p. 64.

"I have no conscience . . . Adolf Hitler." Rauschning, p. 78.

"It was Goering's role to assure the wealthy . . ." Turner, *Business*, p. 132.

The toy bombing, Francois-Poncet, p. 217. The Duke and Duchess of Windsor had a similar experience, Schmidt, pp. 74–5 and 231.

"When bombs did begin falling . . ." Semmler says that through 1942, the crowds still generally greeted Goering with favor but as Berlin came under constant attack the mood changed, p. 97.

Goering passing out in the middle of his own speech, Speer, p. 266.

"He began painting his fingernails . . ." *Ibid.*, pp. 259–60.

Hitler rendered speechless by Goering as a Maharaja, Linge, Oct. 22, 1955.

". . . olive drab . . ." Speer, p. 474.

"Lick my ass." *Gilbert, Nuremberg*, p. 113.

Chapter 34: Joseph Goebbels

The opening quote is as cited by Shirer, p. 129.

"I demand . . . Nazi Party!" Strasser, p. 86. For the refutation of this, see *Dr. Goebbels: His Life and Death*, by Roger Manvell and Heinrich Fraenkel (Simon and Schuster, 1960) p. 53.

"He spoils me . . . Hitler!" *Ibid.*, pp. 61–2.

The radio and record stratagems, Hanfstaengl, p. 201.

"Yes, my Fuehrer . . . very feeble." Rauschning, p. 48.

Goebbels taking credit for the Fuehrer myth, Semmler, pp. 56–7.

"Goebbels' hatred of Jews . . . to a bull." *Ibid.*, p. 98.

"Don't you want . . . the screen." *Ibid.*, p. 194.

"At the last minute I couldn't do it." Linge, Oct. 27, 1955.

". . . some evidence the oldest child . . . struggled to save her life." O'Donnell, pp. 260–1.

Chapter 35: Heinrich Himmler

The opening quote is from Trevor-Roper, pp. 97–8.

"... Himmler kept a dossier ..." Maser, pp. 10–11.

"One day Himmler ... biggest industrialists." *Secret Conversations*, entry for 12 Nov 41, p. 105.

"Except Hitler ... fear of Himmler." Semmler, p. 179.

"... the skull of an infant." Goudsmit, p. 124.

For the efforts at mind control, Schellenberg, p. 15.

"Most of you ... in love to our people." *The Nazi Years: A Documentary History*, Ed. by Joachim Remak (Prentice-Hall, Inc., 1969) pp. 159–60.

"... Eisenhower might employ him as Chief of Police for postwar Europe." Speer, p. 486.

"He also began exploring the possibility ..." Schellenberg, pp. 392–404. Also, Folk Bernadotte wrote a short memoir about these days, *The Curtain Falls* (Alfred A. Knopf, 1945).

Himmler's death is described in detail by witnesses in *After the Battle* Magazine, No. 14, pp. 34–5.

BIBLIOGRAPHY

Alliluyeva, Svetlana, *Twenty Letters to a Friend*. Translated by Priscilla Johnson McMillan (London: Hutchinson & Co.) 1967.

Barnes, James J. and Patricia P., *Hitler's Mein Kampf in Britain and America: A Publishing History* (New York: Cambridge University Press) 1980.

Bernadotte, Folk, *The Curtain Falls* (New York: Alfred A. Knopf) 1945.

Bezymenski, Lev, *The Death of Adolf Hitler: Unknown Documents from Soviet Archives* (New York: Harcourt, Brace & World) 1968.

Bloch, Dr. Eduard, as told to J. D. Ratcliff, "My Patient, Hitler," *Collier's* magazine (March 15, 1941) p. 11 *et seq.*; (March 22, 1941) p. 69 *et seq.*

Breo, Dennis L., "Hitler's Final Days Recalled by Physician." Interview with Dr. Ernst Gunther Schenck. *American Medical News* (October 11, 1985) p. 1 *et. seq.*

Bullock, Alan, *Hitler: A Study in Tyranny—Completely*

Revised Edition (New York: Harper & Row) 1962.

Byrnes, James F., *Speaking Freely* (New York: Harper & Brothers) 1947.

Chipp, Herschel B., *Theories of Modern Art: A Source Book by Artists and Critics* (Berkeley: University of California Press) 1968.

Cole, Wayne S., *Charles A. Lindbergh and the Battle Against American Intervention in World War II* (New York: Harcourt Brace Jovanovich) 1974.

Collier, Richard, *Duce! The Rise and Fall of Benito Mussolini* (New York: The Viking Press) 1971.

Dawidowicz, Lucy S., *The War Against the Jews 1933–1945* (New York: Bantam Books, Inc.) 1976.

Delmer, Sefton, *Black Boomerang* (London: Secker & Warburg) 1962.

Dodd, William E., Jr. and Martha Dodd, Ed., *Ambassador Dodd's Diary* (New York: Harcourt, Brace & World) 1941.

Ellsberg, Daniel, "The Political Uses of Madness," one of a series, *The Act of Coercion: A Study of Threats in Economic Conflict and War*, Lowell Institute Lectures, Boston, 1959. Unpublished.

Fest, Joachim C., *Hitler*. Translated by Richard and Clara Winston (New York: Harcourt Brace Jovanovich) 1973.

Flanner, Janet, *Janet Flanner's World* (New York: Harcourt Brace Jovanovich) 1979.

Fleming, Gerald, *Hitler and the Final Solution* (London: Hamish Hamilton) 1985.

Francois-Poncet, Andre, *The Fateful Years: Memoirs of a French Ambassador in Berlin 1933–1938*. Translated from the French by Jacques Le Clercq (London: Victor Gollancz) 1949.

Friedlander, Saul, *Prelude to Downfall: Hitler and the United States, 1939–1941*. Translated from the French by Aline B. and Alexander Werth (New York: Alfred A. Knopf) 1967.

Gelderman, Carol, *Henry Ford: The Wayward Capitalist* (New York: The Dial Press) 1981.

Gilbert, G. M., *Nuremberg Diary* (New York: Farrar, Straus) 1947.

———*The Psychology of Dictatorship* (New York: Ronald Press) 1950.

Goebbels, Joseph, *The Goebbels Diaries, 1939–1941*. Translated and edited by Fred Taylor (New York: G. P. Putnam's Sons) 1983.

Goudsmit, Samuel A., *Alsos* (London: Sigma Books) 1947.

Grosshans, Henry, *Hitler and the Artists* (New York: Holmes & Meier) 1983.

Grunberger, Richard, *The Twelve Year Reich: A Social History of Nazi Germany 1933–1945* (New York: Holt, Rinehart and Winston) 1971.

Grunfeld, Frederic V., *The Hitler File: A Social History of Germany and the Nazis, 1918–1945* (New York: Random House) 1974.

Hale, Oron James, "Adolf Hitler: Taxpayer," *American Historical Review* (July 1955) pp. 830–41.

Hanfstaengl, Ernst, *Unheard Witness* (Philadelphia: J. B Lippincott Co.) 1957.

Hanisch, Reinhold, "I Was Hitler's Buddy," *The New Republic* (April 5, 1939) pp. 239–42; (April 12, 1939) pp. 270–2; (April 19, 1939) pp. 297–300.

Harris, Robert, *Selling Hitler* (New York: Pantheon Books) 1986.

Hart, B. H. Liddell, *The German Generals Talk* (New York: William Morrow & Co.) 1948.

Hart-Davis, Duff, *Hitler's Games: The 1936 Olympics* (New York: Harper & Row) 1986.

Heiden, Konrad, *Der Fuehrer: Hitler's Rise to Power*. Translated by Ralph Manheim (Boston: Houghton Mifflin Co.) 1944.

————*A History of National Socialism*. Translated from the German (New York: Alfred A. Knopf) 1940.

————*Hitler, a Biography* (London: Constable) 1936.

Hitler, Adolf, *My New Order*. Edited with Commentary by Raoul de Roussy de Sales (New York: Reynal & Hitchcock) 1941.

Hitler's Secret Conversations 1941–1944, With an Introductory essay on The Mind of Adolf Hitler by H. R. Trevor-Roper. Translated by Norman Cameron and R. H. Stevens (New York: Farrar, Straus and Young) 1953.

Hoffmann, Peter, *History of the German Resistance 1933–1945*. Translated from the German by Richard Barry (Cambridge: The MIT Press) 1977.

————*Hitler's Personal Security* (London: The Macmillan Press) 1979.

Howe, Ellic, *Urania's Children* (London: William Kimber) 1967.

Infield, Glenn B., *Hitler's Secret Life* (New York: Stein and Day) 1979.

Irving, David, *Hitler's War* (New York: The Viking Press) 1977.

————*The Secret Diaries of Hitler's Doctor* (New

York: Macmillan Publishing Co.) 1983.

————*The War Path: Hitler's Germany 1933–1939* (New York: The Viking Press) 1978.

Jetzinger, Franz, *Hitler's Youth*. Translated from the German by Lawrence Wilson (London: Hutchinson) 1958.

Khrushchev, Nikita, *Khrushchev Remembers*, Commentary and Notes by Edward Crankshaw. Translated and Edited by Strobe Talbot (Boston: Little, Brown and Company) 1970.

Kirkpatrick, Ivone, *The Inner Circle* (London: The Macmillan Press) 1959.

Kubizek, August, *Young Hitler: The Story of Our Friendship*. Translated from the German by E. V. Anderson (London: Allan Wingate) 1954.

Langer, Walter C., *The Mind of Adolf Hitler: The Secret Wartime Report* (New York: Basic Books, Inc.) 1972.

Lewin, Ronald, *Hitler's Mistakes* (New York: William Morrow & Co.) 1984.

Lifton, Robert Jay, *The Nazi Doctors: Medical Killing and the Psychology of Genocide* (New York: Basic Books, Inc.) 1986.

Linge, Heinz, "Valet Begins Own Story of Hitler's Private Life," Chicago *Daily News* (October 22, 1955) p. 6 *et seq.*

Ludecke, Kurt G. W., *I Knew Hitler: The Story of a Nazi Who Escaped the Blood Purge* (New York: Charles Scribner's Sons) 1938.

Mandell, Richard D., *The Nazi Olympics* (London: The Macmillan Press) 1971.

Manvell, Roger and Fraenkel, Heinrich, *Dr. Goebbels:*

His Life and Death (New York: Simon and Schuster)
1960.

Maser, Werner, *Hitler: Legend, Myth and Reality.*
Translated from the German by Peter and Betty Ross.
(New York: Harper & Row) 1973.

————*Hitler's Letters and Notes.* Translated by Richard
Pomerans (London: William Heinemannn, Ltd.)
1974.

Mason, Herbert Molloy, Jr., *To Kill the Devil: The Attempts on the Life of Adolf Hitler* (New York: W. W.
Norton & Co.) 1978.

McKale, Donald M., *Hitler: The Survival Myth* (New
York: Stein and Day) 1981.

Murphy, Robert, *Diplomat Among Warriors* (Garden
City, New York: Doubleday & Co.) 1964.

Musmanno, Michael A., *Ten Days to Die* (Garden City,
New York: Doubleday & Co.) 1950.

Nelson, Walter Henry, *Small Wonder: The Amazing
Story of the Volkswagen* (Boston: Little, Brown and
Company) 1965.

O'Donnell, James P., *The Bunker: The History of the
Reich Chancellery Group* (Boston: Houghton Mifflin
Co.) 1978.

Oechsner, Frederick, *This Is the Enemy* (Boston: Little,
Brown and Co.) 1942.

OSS Source Book. These are the interviews and notes
compiled under the direction of Dr. Walter Langer,
working for the Office of Strategic Services (see p.
239, Langer, Walter, *The Mind of Adolf Hitler*).

Payne, Robert, *Eyewitness: A Personal Account of a Tumultuous Decade, 1937–46* (Garden City, New York:
Doubleday & Co.) 1972.

————*The Life and Death of Adolf Hitler* (New York: Praeger Publishers) 1973.

Price, G. Ward, *I Know These Dictators* (New York: Henry Holt and Company) 1938.

Rauschning, Hermann, *The Voice of Destruction* (New York: G. P. Putnam's Sons) 1940.

Rector, Frank, *The Nazi Extermination of Homosexuals* (New York: Stein and Day) 1981.

Remak, Joachim, Ed., *The Nazi Years: A Documentary History* (Englewood Cliffs, New Jersey: Prentice-Hall, Inc.) 1967.

Roberts, Stephen H., *The House That Hitler Built* (New York: Harper & Brothers) 1938.

Rosenfeld, Alvin H., *Imagining Hitler* (Bloomington: Indiana University Press) 1985.

Salisbury, Harrison E., *Without Fear or Favor* (New York: Times Books) 1980.

Schellenberg, Walter, *The Labyrinth*. Translated by Louis Hagen (New York: Harper & Brothers) 1956.

Schlabrendorff, Fabian von, *The Secret War Against Hitler*. Translated by Hilda Simon (New York: Pittman Publishing) 1965.

Schmidt, Dr. Paul, *Hitler's Interpreter*. Edited by R. H. C. Steed (New York: The Macmillan Co.) 1951.

Schramm, Percy Ernst, *Hitler: The Man and the Military Leader*. Translated by Donald S. Detwiler (Chicago: Quadrangle Books) 1971.

The Secret Life of Adolf Hitler, a book based on a television documentary of the same name, produced for WPIX by William Cooper, Jr. and Walter D. Engels.

Text adapted from the script by Eldorous L. Dayton (New York: The Citadel Press) 1960.

Semmler, Rudolf, *Goebbels: The Man Next to Hitler* (London: Westhouse) 1947.

Shirer, William, *Berlin Diary* (New York: Alfred A. Knopf) 1941.

————*The Nightmare Years* (Boston: Little, Brown and Co.) 1985.

————*The Rise and Fall of the Third Reich: A History of Nazi Germany* (New York: Simon and Schuster) 1960.

Sklar, Dusty, *Gods & Beasts: The Nazis and the Occult* (New York: Thomas Y. Crowell Company) 1977.

Smith, Bradley F., *Adolf Hitler: His Family, Childhood and Youth* (Stanford: Hoover Institution Press) 1967.

Smith, Truman, *Berlin Alert: The Memoirs and Reports of Truman Smith*, Ed. by Robert Hessen (Stanford: Hoover Institution Press) 1984.

Sognnaes, Reidar F. "Dental Evidence in the Postmortem Identification of Adolf Hitler, Eva Braun, and Martin Bormann," *Legal Medicine Annual, 1976* (Englewood Cliffs, New Jersey: Prentice-Hall, Inc.) pp. 173–235.

Speer, Albert, *Inside the Third Reich*. Translated by Richard and Clara Winston (New York: The Macmillan Co.) 1970.

————*Playboy* magazine, "Playboy Interview: Albert Speer" (July, 1971) p. 69 *et seq.*

————*Spandau: The Secret Diaries*. Translated by Richard and Clara Winston (New York: Macmillan Publishing Co.) 1976.

Strasser, Otto, *Hitler and I*. Translated by Gwenda David and Eric Mosbacher (Boston: Houghton Mifflin Co.) 1940.

Thyssen, Fritz, *I Paid Hitler*. Translated by Cesar Saerchinger (New York: Farrar & Rinehart, Inc.) 1941.

Toland, John, *Adolf Hitler* (Garden City, New York: Doubleday & Co.) 1976.

Turner, Henry Ashby, Jr., *German Big Business and the Rise of Hitler* (New York: Oxford University Press) 1985.

———, Ed. *Hitler—Memoirs of a Confidant*. Translated by Ruth Hein. (New Haven: Yale University Press) 1985.

Waite, Robert G. L., *The Psychopathic God* (New York: Basic Books, Inc.) 1977.

Winterbotham, F. W. *The Nazi Connection* (New York: Harper & Row) 1978.

Wood, Jonathan, *The VW Beetle* (London: Motor Racing Publications) 1979.

Chronology

1889

April 20   Adolf Hitler born at 6:30 p.m. in the town of Braunau am Inn, Austria. Despite a legend to the contrary, his name at birth is Hitler, not Schicklgruber. See chapter 4.

1894

March 24   Edmund Hitler, Adolf's brother, born. He will die in 1900, age 5, of measles.

1896

January 21   Paula, Hitler's sister, born. She will survive Adolf, living until 1960. He will also be outlived by his half brother Alois, Jr. (b. 1882) and half sister Angela (b. 1883). See chapter 12.

1903

January 3   Hitler's father, Alois, dies.

1905

January   The fifteen-year-old Hitler, a regular operagoer, sees Wagner's *Rienzi* and is inspired to a first glimpse of his "political destiny." See chapter 21.

Until now Hitler has imagined himself becoming an artist, an ambition to which he returns but will never pursue with any discipline.

1907

October   Hitler takes the examination for admission to the painting school of the Academy of Fine Art in Vienna. He passes the first part of the exam but fails the second and is denied admission. See chapter 22.

December 21   Hitler's mother, Klara, dies.

1908

Throughout his years in Vienna, Hitler manages to make a living producing decorative paintings, postcards and advertising posters.

During this period he becomes an avid reader of anti-Semitic pamphlets, and it is in the summer of this year that he makes his first overt political decision,

| | joining an organization called The Anti-Semite Union. See chapter 31. |
| September | Hitler again takes the entrance exam for the Fine Arts Academy. This time he fails the first part and is not allowed to take the second. |

1909

| April 20 | Hitler's twentieth birthday; he is now required to register for military service, which he never does. He changes his place of residence frequently hereafter. |

1910

| | Some time in the spring of this year, Hitler sees a film, *The Tunnel*, which awakens him to the power of oratory in politics. See chapter 18. |

1913

| May | Motivated in large part by his desire to avoid serving in the Austrian army, Hitler now moves to Munich, Germany. |

1914

| January | He is arrested by the Munich police, at the request of the Austrians, and is sent back to Austria. |
| February 5 | Military doctors judge him too weak to bear arms. He returns to Munich. |

August 1   World War I begins.

August 16   Hitler joins the German Army. Although he is an Austrian by birth he has always regarded himself as German by blood.

October 28   Hitler's regiment goes into combat.

                    Hitler is soon made a dispatch runner, a dangerous job that he will perform throughout the war with consistent courage. In later years his comrades will recall that although they soon grew to detest the war, Hitler seemed to thrive on it. See chapter 10.

December 2   Hitler receives the Iron Cross, Second Class.

1915

February 5   Hitler writes a letter home in which he tells of a bullet that tore off his sleeve but left him unharmed. This and other close calls help convince him he is being saved for a special, historic destiny.

1916

October 5   Wounded by shell splinters, hospitalized for two months.

1917

September 17   Awarded the Military Service Cross, Third Class.

Despite his years of service, courage and competence, Hitler is never promoted beyond his lowly corporal's rank (corresponding to private first class in the U.S. system). His superiors judge he lacks leadership potential.

1918

May 9   Awarded a regimental citation for outstanding bravery.

August 4   Awarded the Iron Cross, First Class, an important medal. He will always be reticent about how and why it was awarded, loath to reveal that the officer who recommended him was a Jew.

October 14   Caught in a poison gas attack during a battle, he is hospitalized with temporary blindness.

November 10   Germany surrenders.

November 19   Released from the hospital, he is sent to a regiment in Munich.

1919

He keeps clear of a series of uprisings and repressions that break out in Munich, then becomes a political lecturer for the army.

June 28   In Paris, the Versailles Treaty is

signed, formally ending World War I.
Its terms include reparations to be paid
by the Germans to the Allies. These
payments will become an onerous bur-
den, and resentment of them will be
skillfully exploited by Hitler and the
Nazis.

September 12   Hitler is sent to observe a meeting
conducted by an utterly obscure group,
the German Workers Party. Disagree-
ing with a speaker, he leaps to his feet
and delivers a ferocious impromptu rebuttal. The members are deeply impressed.

September 16   Asked by his army superiors to prepare a paper on the "Jewish question,"
Hitler responds with his first known
writing on the subject. In it he appeals
for an anti-Semitism that is rational
rather than emotional. What is needed,
he argues, is a coolly systematic policy
leading to "the total removal of all
Jews from our midst." See chapter 31.

October 19   Although he did not apply for membership in the German Workers Party,
he has received a membership card
and agrees to join.

1920
February 20   The German Workers Party changes

its name to the National Socialist German Workers Party—Nazi. Hitler wants a shorter name but is not yet powerful enough to get his way. See chapter 5.

February 24   The Nazis announce their basic platform, "The 25 Points." Much of this will be discarded in years to come, but its demand that Jews be deprived of their citizenship will eventually become law under Hitler's rule.

March 31   Hitler resigns from the army.

Tireless in his oratory and relentlessly ambitious, he begins to dominate the Party. Through countless fiery public meetings, the Party begins to attract attention and members.

December 17   At Hitler's insistence, the Nazis buy a Munich newspaper and convert it into their Party organ, the *Volkischer Beobachter*. In time, they will publish papers throughout Germany, promoting their propaganda and producing income both for the Party and for Hitler personally. See chapter 24.

1921
July 11   Hitler resigns from the Nazi Party. He has been waging a fight against those who want to ally or merge the Nazis

with other nationalistic parties. He
fears his power will be diminished.
Also, he complains that the other parties are not resolute enough in their hatred of Jews.

July 29   As he calculated, his resignation causes
a crisis. He agrees to return, on the con-
dition that he is accorded complete
obedience. For the first time he is
hailed as the Party's *Fuehrer* (Leader).
See chapter 4.

September 4   He announces the formation of the
S.A., the brown-shirted Storm Troop-
ers who will quite literally help him
fight his way to national power.

1922
June 24   He is imprisoned for a month for using
his Storm Troopers to break up a po-
litical meeting and beat up the speaker.

Because of the constant agitation he
foments, the government considers de-
porting him. This is possible because
he is still a citizen of Austria, not Germany. Nothing comes of the plan, in
large part because many officials are
sympathetic to his call for the reestab-
lishment of German power.

October 14–15   Hitler takes his Storm Troopers to a
German Day celebration in the town

of Coburg, a Socialist stronghold. The result is a street riot that approaches the proportions of a pitched battle. The Nazis will count this as one of their great early victories.

October 20   A U.S. military attache in Germany, Capt. Truman Smith, becomes the first American to interview Hitler. He notes that although other Nazis hint their anti-Semitism is only for propaganda purposes, Hitler is in deadly earnest.

November   Hermann Goering hears Hitler speak, then introduces himself and soon goes to work for him. He will become most famous as head of the new German Air Force, and for his debaucheries. See chapter 33.

December 20   The *New York Times* reports that a picture of Henry Ford hangs by Hitler's desk. Hitler admires Ford for sponsoring anti-Semitic propaganda and has Ford's book, *The International Jew* distributed by the Nazi Party. See chapter 6.

1923

January 11   Because Germany has fallen behind on reparations due under the Versailles Treaty, France and Belgium occupy the Ruhr Valley, Germany's coal and steel region. This inflames patriotic nationalism throughout Germany. At the same time, a devastating inflation sweeps the economy. People are desperate, and in these conditions the Nazis thrive.

Hitler lays plans for an overthrow of the Bavarian State government in southern Germany and a march on Berlin to seize national power.

November 8   He begins his revolution by firing a bullet into the ceiling of a Munich beer hall.

November 9   Marching to the Munich Town Hall, Hitler and his Storm Troopers are confronted by police, who open fire. Sixteen Nazis and three police are killed in the melee. Hitler suffers a dislocated shoulder and flees. The so-called Beer Hall Putsch is over.

November 11   Found hiding at a friend's house, Hitler is arrested and jailed at Landsberg Prison. His cell fills with presents from well-wishers and he is treated as a hero by prison personnel.

1924
February 26–
April 1   Hitler's trial. He defends himself with vigorous self-righteousness and receives international attention.

April 1	Sentenced to five years imprisonment.
	In jail he begins writing *Mein Kampf*, his autobiography-manifesto. See chapter 3.
May 4	Elections for the Reichstag, the national assembly. Because the Nazi Party is temporarily banned, its candidates, who are participating for the first time, must run under different designations. They do moderately well, winning 32 seats.
December 7	The Allies have relented considerably on reparations and in another Reichstag election, the Nazis are reduced to 14 seats.
December 20	Despite having four years left to serve, Hitler is released in time to be home for Christmas.

1925

April 7	He orders the creation of a special, personal bodyguard detachment within the Storm Troopers. This new unit will become the S.S., the most powerful and hated of all Nazi organizations.
April 30	Hitler renounces his Austrian citizenship, a legal maneuver making it difficult for him to be deported. He will not acquire German citizenship until 1932.

July 18   Volume I of *Mein Kampf* is published.

                      In the summer of this year, Joseph
                      Goebbels, who will become the noto-
                      rious Minister for Propaganda and En-
                      lightenment, meets Hitler. He regards
                      himself as more radical than Hitler but
                      soon becomes one of his most faithful
                      servants. See chapter 34.

December 11   Volume II of *Mein Kampf* is pub-
                      lished. Although *Mein Kampf* does not
                      sell well at first, it will eventually help
                      make Hitler a millionaire. See chapter
                      24.

1928

May 20   Reichstag elections—the Nazis do
                      poorly. The German economy is steady-
                      ing; employment is up.

                      Late in the year, the economy falters
                      and unemployment begins an ominous
                      climb.

1929

January 9   Heinrich Himmler is made head of the
                      S.S. See chapter 35.

June 7   The Young Plan announced, an agree-
                      ment which further reduces the pay-
                      ments Germany is to make to the
                      World War I victors, but even this is
                      a disappointment to many Germans.

June 23	Coburg becomes the first city in Germany to elect a majority of Nazis to its City Council.
September	Hitler buys the mountain cottage outside Berchtesgaden, which he will eventually expand into the Berghof. See chapter 23.
October	Hitler meets Eva Braun, whom he will marry a day before their joint suicide in 1945. See chapter 11.
October 24	In New York, the collapse of the stock market triggers the worldwide Great Depression.

1930

January 23	For the first time, a Nazi is made a State Minister, in Thuringa.
February 24	A Storm Trooper and reputed pimp named Horst Wessel dies in a Berlin street fight. Hitler and Goebbels make him the official Party martyr and adopt a song he wrote as the Nazi anthem.
July 5	Hitler buys the building in Munich that will become known as the Brown House, Nazi Party headquarters.
September 14	The Nazis score sensationally well in the Reichstag elections, becoming the second most powerful party in the assembly.

1931

September 17   Geli Raubal, Hitler's niece, shoots herself. See chapter 11.

September 25   Hitler declares he is revolted by the thought of eating meat and adopts a vegetarian diet. See chapter 14.

During this year, the Nazis win seats in local elections throughout Germany.

1932

January 27   Hitler speaks to the Industry Club in Dusseldorf, presenting the Nazis as supportive of big business. Formerly, Hitler had declared himself an anti-capitalist seeking the nationalization of industry and the abolishing of interest income.

February 25   So that he will be eligible to run for the presidency, Hitler has himself made a German citizen through bureaucratic machinations.

April 10   Loses presidential bid, but wins over 36 percent of the popular vote.

July 31   Reichstag elections. Although the Nazis do not win a majority of the seats, they gain enough to become the single most powerful party.

August 13   Hitler, who wanted to be appointed

Chancellor, is offered the Vice-Chancellorship. He refuses.

1933

January 30   As the climax of a complex political deal, which is supposed to harness Hitler to the service of the established system, he is appointed Chancellor of Germany.

February 27   A fire of mysterious origin ravages the Reichstag building. Although the Nazis may not have set the fire, Hitler uses it as an excuse to ask for extraordinary, anti-democratic powers. To insure getting the legislation he wants, many opposing Reichstag members are arrested or frightened into hiding.

The single most important bill establishing the dictatorship, the Enabling Act, will be passed on March 24.

March   Dachau concentration camp established, for incarceration of anyone deemed a threat to Nazi rule. In time, a network of these camps will be established, and they will be used for mass exterminations, principally of Jews.

March 12   Hitler announces that henceforth the Nazi Party flag—the swastika—will fly alongside the German national flag.

April 1–4   The first national boycott against Jew-
                   ish businesses.

April 7   Jews are eliminated from the Civil Ser-
                   vice. This law is the first of hundreds
                   that will systematically exclude
                   German Jews from the professions,
                   commerce, even athletics and the use of
                   recreational facilities such as beaches
                   and ski slopes. See chapter 31.

June–July   All political parties—other than the
                   Nazis—are dissolved.

July 6   Hitler announces that the Nazi Party
                   has become the State.

October 12   Germany pulls out of the League of
                   Nations.

November 12   In a national referendum, over 95 per-
                   cent of voters give their approval to
                   Hitler and his policies.

1934
February 19   The military adopts swastika insignia.

June 14   Hitler flies to Venice for his first meet-
                   ing with Mussolini. He makes a poor
                   impression on the Italian dictator, who
                   concludes that Hitler is somewhat de-
                   ranged. See chapter 25.

June 30–July 1   The Blood Purge, directed principally
                   against the leadership of the S.A. but

its victims include a wide range of real and imagined Hitler opponents. After this, the S.S. will become increasingly important. See chapter 35.

July 25   The Austrian Nazis murder the Austrian Chancellor. Outraged at the possibility of a German takeover, Mussolini mobilizes troops on the border. Hitler backs down, disavows the Austrian Nazis.

August 2   President Hindenburg dies. Hitler abolishes the office of President, takes over its duties and creates a new, all-encompassing title for himself: "Fuehrer and Reich Chancellor." See chapter 4.

Also on this day, all members of the military are required to swear an oath of loyalty to Hitler personally.

September 4–10   At the annual Party celebration at Nuremberg, Hitler announces there will be no more revolutions in Germany for a thousand years.

1935

January   At the Berlin Auto Show Hitler announces that Germany will soon produce a car the ordinary citizen can afford, a Volkswagen ("People's Car"). See chapter 7.

March 16   Hitler reintroduces the draft, a key part
                of a substantial military buildup. Ger-
                many will no longer abide by the Ver-
                sailles Treaty.

Sept. 10–17   At the annual Nuremberg rally, Hitler
                decrees that henceforth the Nazi swas-
                tika flag will be the sole national flag
                of Germany.

                Also announced are the notorious Nu-
                remberg Laws, which deprive German
                Jews of their citizenship and forbid
                marriage between Jews and non-Jews.
                See chapter 31.

1936
February 6   Hitler opens the Winter Olympic
                Games.

March 7   He sends troops into the Rhineland, on
                the border with France. Under the
                terms ending World War I, no troops
                are to be in this area, but Hitler's gam-
                ble pays off. The French do not op-
                pose him. See chapter 20.

July 16   Spanish Civil War begins. Hitler and
                Mussolini back Franco.

August 1   In Berlin, Hitler opens the Summer
                Olympic Games. Despite the fact that
                he originally opposed them, the Games
                prove a great Nazi propaganda suc-
                cess. See chapter 29.

October 21   Hitler and Mussolini reach an agreement that forms the basis for the "Axis," the alliance of Fascist countries.

November 25   Germany signs an alliance with Japan.

1937

April 26   In Spain, assisting Franco, German bombers destroy the town of Guernica, field-testing the techniques they will use with devastating effect as part of their *Blitzkrieg* (Lightning War) in the beginning of World War II.

July 19   Hitler opens the House of German Art. Concurrently, the Exhibition of Degenerate Art begins, which becomes one of the most successful art shows in history. See chapter 22.

Sept. 25–29   Mussolini visits Hitler and is impressed by Germany's enormously increased military power. He revises his opinion of Hitler.

November 5   In a secret meeting with his top commanders, Hitler reveals his plans to invade Austria and Czechoslovakia.

1938

March 11   Mussolini agrees not to oppose Hitler's invasion of Austria.

March 12   German troops enter Austria. The
                  event is more a parade than an inva-
                  sion. Hitler is welcomed by cheering
                  crowds.

September 30   As the culmination of a series of meet-
                  ings, British Prime Minister Chamber-
                  lain agrees not to protest German
                  seizure of the Sudetenland portion of
                  Czechoslovakia, in return for Hitler's
                  promise to give up aggression in Eu-
                  rope.

October 1   German troops occupy the Sudeten-
                  land.

November 9–10   "Crystal Night," named for the shat-
                  tered window glass knocked out of
                  Jewish shops, homes, and synagogues
                  by rioters throughout the country. Al-
                  though Nazi Storm Troopers have rou-
                  tinely terrorized Jews for years, this is
                  the first government-sanctioned po-
                  grom against German Jews since the
                  Middle Ages. See chapter 31.

1939

March 15   Facing the threat of imminent attack,
                  the government of Czechoslovakia
                  agrees to a bloodless invasion of the
                  remainder of the country. Hitler is in
                  Prague by the end of the day.

May 22   Germany and Italy sign the so-called
                  "Pact of Steel," a military alliance.

August 23	The Hitler-Stalin Pact is signed. This includes secret clauses that allow the Soviet Union to seize the Baltic countries, and divide Poland between the Soviet Union and Germany. See chapter 25.
August 31	To create an excuse for the invasion of Poland, the Germans stage a fake attack by Polish troops on the border. See chapter 20.
September 1	Germany invades Poland.
September 3	Britain and France declare war on Germany.
September 17	The Soviet army invades Poland from the east.
September 21	Hitler orders Jews in German-occupied areas of Poland rounded up and held in ghettos. This will facilitate their systematic extermination.

1940

| April 9 | Germany attacks Denmark and Norway. |
| April 27 | Hitler issues orders for the establishment of the death camp complex at Auschwitz, Poland. Of the six million Jews who will be murdered by the Nazis, two million will die here. |

May 10	Germany attacks the Netherlands, Luxembourg, Belgium and France. In England, Winston Churchill becomes Prime Minister.
May 28	The British Army is evacuated from the European continent, at Dunkirk.
June 10	Italy declares war on France and Britain.
June 22	The French surrender. One of Hitler's sycophantic subordinates creates a new title for him: "Greatest Commander of All Time" (abbreviated as "*Grofaz*"). See chapter 4.
July 10–October 31	The Battle of Britain, an attempt by Germany to destroy the Royal Air Force, a necessary prerequisite to invading Britain. The Germans fail.
October 23	Hitler meets with Franco, the Spanish dictator, who politely but firmly refuses to cooperate in an attack on the British fortress at Gibraltar. See chapter 25.

1941

February	Germany begins operations in North Africa, in support of the Italians against the British.
April 6	Germany attacks Greece and Yugoslavia, in support of the Italians.

May 10   Rudolf Hess, Hitler's deputy, flies to Scotland. See chapter 27.

June 1   Germany attacks Crete.

June 22   Germany invades the Soviet Union.

December 7   The Japanese attack Pearl Harbor.

December 8   The United States declares war on Japan.

December 11   Hitler declares war on the U.S. See chapter 26.

December 19   Dissatisfied with progress of the war in Russia, Hitler assumes personal command of the army.

1942

January 20   The Wannsee Conference, to coordinate civilian, Party and military resources for the Final Solution, the murder of all the Jews in Europe.

April 26   Hitler declares himself Supreme Law Lord. See chapter 4.

July 3   The Battle of El Alamein, which marks the beginning of the end for the German-Italian campaign in North Africa.

November 22   A huge German force is surrounded and trapped at Stalingrad, in the Soviet Union.

1943

January 14–26   Meeting at Casablanca, the Allied
                     leaders agree to accept nothing less
                     than the unconditional surrender of
                     Nazi Germany.

February 3   The German army at Stalingrad sur-
                     renders. This marks the turning of the
                     tide in the East.

April 7–June 16   The destruction of the Warsaw Ghetto
                     by the Nazis, despite a desperate resis-
                     tance by the Jews there.

May 13   German defeat at Tunis, the end of the
                     war in North Africa.

July 10   The Allies land in Sicily.

July 25   Mussolini arrested by former support-
                     ers.

September 12   The rescue of Mussolini. See chapter
                     25.

October 13   Italy declares war on Germany.

November 28–   Roosevelt and Churchill meet Stalin
December 1   for the first time, in Tehran. Discus-
                     sions include coordinating the eastern
                     and western fronts in Europe.

1944

January 4–5   The Soviet Army, having thrown back
                     the Germans, crosses into Poland.

January 22	The Allies land on the Italian mainland, at Anzio.
June 6	The Allies land at Normandy, in northern France. D-Day.
June 15	The first V-1 "buzz bombs" are launched against London. See chapter 28.
July 20	Hitler is only wounded by the bomb planted in an assassination attempt by high-ranking officers. See chapter 30.
August 25	The Allies enter Paris.
September 8	V-2 ballistic missile attacks begin. See chapter 28.
December 16	The Battle of the Bulge launched by Hitler, an attempt to stem the Allied advance in the west. It fails.

1945

January	In the east, the Russians enter Germany.
January 16	Hitler returns to Berlin from his military HQ in Prussia and moves into his underground Chancellery bunker.
February 4–11	Roosevelt, Churchill, Stalin meet at Yalta, agree on occupied rule of Germany. Also, the Soviets agree to participate in the United Nations.

March–April	Hitler issues a series of decrees ordering that everything of any value is to be destroyed rather than fall into enemy hands, even if this means the German people will starve after the war.
April 12	President Roosevelt dies. Goebbels and Hitler are ecstatic, interpreting this as a mystical sign that Germany is to win the war after all. A horoscope is consulted. See chapter 27.
April 21	The Soviets reach the outskirts of Berlin, start fighting their way in.
April 23	Hitler decides Hermann Goering is a traitor, strips him of all his rank and offices. See chapter 33.
April 28	Hitler declares Heinrich Himmler a traitor, orders him arrested. See chapter 35.
April 29	Hitler and Eva Braun marry. Later, Hitler dictates his "Political Testament," in which he blames the Jews for starting World War II.
April 30	Hitler and Eva kill themselves. Their bodies are doused with gasoline and set aflame, but do not burn completely. The remains are later found and their identities confirmed by the Soviets. See chapter 32.

INDEX